Self-Directed Complex PTSD Exercises for Women

Self-Directed Complex PTSD Exercises for Women

Mind-Body Practices for Safety, Stability, and Self-Love

DEBBIE MISSUD, LMHC-D

ZEITGEIST • NEW YORK

This book discusses trauma, abuse, and related mental health challenges, which may be distressing for some readers. Please engage at your own pace and seek support if needed.

Zeitgeist™
An imprint and division of Penguin Random House LLC
1745 Broadway, New York, NY 10019
zeitgeistpublishing.com
penguinrandomhouse.com

ISBN: 9798217150984

Printed in the United States of America
1st Printing

Illustrations by Shutterstock.com/Rucula, Shutterstock.com/TWINS DESIGN STUDIO
Cover design by Erin Yeung
Interior design by Emma Hall
Author photograph © by Gianna Carly
Edited by Erin Nelson

The authorized representative in the EU for product safety and compliance is Penguin Random House Ireland, Morrison Chambers, 32 Nassau Street, Dublin D02 YH68, Ireland.
https://eu-contact.penguin.ie

To Ross, for being my secure base and showing me what healthy love looks like. To all my clients, whose courage and resilience remind me daily that we are never defined by what has happened to us.

Contents

A Note *from the* Author

In the same way trauma can appear in many forms, there is no one-size-fits-all approach to healing. Healing is a deeply personal experience, and what supports one person may not resonate with another. This book aims to offer a range of options, allowing you to find approaches that feel helpful, empowering, and safe for you. I encourage you to skip or modify any portion of writing or exercise that feels overwhelming or not aligned with your needs at this time.

The exercises you'll find here are integrative, supporting a wide range of individuals, circumstances, and trauma origins. They are informed by the American Psychological Association's 2024 Guidelines for Working with Adults with Complex Trauma Histories—with a specific focus on the symptoms and lived experiences of women with complex post-traumatic stress disorder (cPTSD)—and adapted to include techniques I've found most effective in my work. This book is thus rooted in both scientific research and direct clinical experience.

As you enter these pages, it's essential to be aware that trauma work carries risk. Engaging with material related to trauma without the support of a licensed mental health professional may lead to an increase in distressing symptoms, such as flashbacks, dissociation, or urges to engage in self-destructive behaviors. If you notice a worsening of symptoms, please discontinue self-guided exercises and consult a licensed professional for guidance.

The information here is not a substitute for psychotherapy or medical treatment. If you are experiencing a mental health crisis and need immediate support, please dial 988. You can also text the Crisis Text Line at 741741. If you have active thoughts of harming yourself or others, please seek help immediately by visiting your nearest comprehensive psychiatric emergency program (CPEP) or your nearest emergency room.

Finally, while this book is intended for anyone who identifies as a woman, I want to acknowledge the unique experiences of transgender women outside the scope of these pages. If you are a transgender woman seeking additional support, I recommend turning to organizations such as the Trevor Project and PFLAG, which provide affirming, specialized resources.

Introduction

Taking control of your healing is a powerful choice. It reflects your strength, resilience, and deep commitment to yourself. Your effort—no matter how smooth or messy the journey may feel—is at the heart of recovery. You are choosing to show up for yourself, to seek safety, to move toward regulation, and to reclaim vitality in your life. That is an act of reclamation no one can take from you.

When living with the impact of complex trauma, the past can seep into every corner of the present. An email from your boss can send you spiraling back to childhood punishments. You may find yourself repeating painful relationship patterns or sabotaging secure connections because intimacy has always felt unsafe. Your body may feel uninhabitable. Coping mechanisms that once protected you now do more harm than good. Anxiety and exhaustion may swing you between extremes, leaving little middle ground. Living with trauma can feel like walking through life with a pair of shoes full of sand—every step is heavier, slower, and more exhausting than it looks to anyone else. But with care and healing, you don't have to carry that grit forever.

When I first entered my clinical practice, trained initially in "behavioral talk therapy," I worked with clients at the level of symptoms. They came with anxiety, relationship struggles, loud inner critics, or harmful coping mechanisms like binge drinking or self-harm. As we went deeper, it became clear that their pain was rooted in unresolved trauma. Intervention skills helped ease the symptoms, but it often felt like putting a bandage on a bullet wound—useful for some relief, but not enough for lasting healing.

Recovering from trauma requires treating the whole person—mind, body, spirit, and environment. It means acknowledging the systems that perpetuate trauma, whether family dynamics, cultural expectations, oppressive structures, or everyday stressors at home or work. Finding peace is far more nuanced than simply "rewiring the brain" or learning to "calm down." Trauma is multilayered, and the body holds memories and stress responses—tied to people, places, and situations—long after the original events.

That's why I pursued training in integrative modalities such as Eye Movement Desensitization and Reprocessing (EMDR), Internal Family Systems (IFS), and Sensorimotor Psychotherapy, and why this book is grounded in a holistic, mind-body approach. Talking about trauma can ease cognitive pain—there's strong evidence for the benefits of verbal processing. But lasting relief requires also exploring how trauma is stored in the body. Movement, breath, and awareness can help regulate the nervous system and create new, safer neural pathways. When we view the mind and body as allies, deeply interconnected, we see how they work together to restore a felt sense of safety.

After years of providing integrative, trauma-focused care, I've witnessed profound shifts in clients—even (and especially) in those who felt dissociated, fearful, depressed, or hopeless. Their journeys were never linear; progress was marked by both breakthroughs and setbacks. The truth is that even after years of therapy and personal growth, people still get dysregulated. The inner critic may return. Relapses can happen. This is normal; it's part of being human.

Healing doesn't mean forgetting the past or never being triggered again. It means learning how to feel safer in your body, more joyful in your spirit, and more hopeful about your future. Every woman I've seen move through this process is proof that it's possible to regain a sense of control, to feel better, and to experience resilience from the inside out.

No one can change what happened to you. But what this book can offer—no matter who you are or what brought you here—is a set of skills to help you understand, process, and cope with trauma's impact. With care and compassion, you'll begin taking steps toward a life that feels more authentic and fulfilling.

How to Use This Book

This book begins with foundational knowledge around cPTSD, especially as it relates to women, and this knowledge is followed by trauma-informed exercises to support the healing journey. Structurally, it looks like this:

Part I offers an overview of complex PTSD—how it impacts women, common symptoms and treatment modalities, and the science behind it.

Part II begins with healing exercises that focus on self-regulation, learning how to feel safer in your body, and gently processing past experiences. It includes tools to start nurturing a more compassionate relationship with yourself.

Part III offers more expansive exercises—helping to integrate trauma into your life story, improve your relationships with others, and widen your capacity for joy. Here, you'll move from resilience to reclamation, learning to live more fully and authentically.

Each part of this book builds on the one before it, so there is good reason to move through it sequentially. However, healing is an individual, nonlinear process—and recovery from complex trauma is, by definition, complex. Move through the material (or hop around) at your preference, but please do so at a pace that respects your nervous system's limits.

If an exercise requires materials such as a yoga mat, journal, or ice, it will be listed up front. Each exercise includes a step-by-step guide with recommendations for how long it might take and how often to practice.

Throughout this book, you'll find many spaces to write and lines to fill on the page. I encourage you to do so. However, some exercises will recommend using a journal or notebook in the "What You Will Need" section. In these cases, the writing space is intentionally minimal so your response can take whatever shape it needs. Even if a notebook isn't specified, you can always use something separate or additional for your thoughts if you prefer (including blank digital templates). These prompts are the start of an ongoing conversation with yourself. Respond in ways that feel most useful to you—whether by writing, thinking, or talking.

Tuning In

"Tuning In" checkpoints are intentionally brief. For deeper self-assessment and support, I encourage you to revisit the full list of questions below:

- How am I feeling in this moment—emotionally, physically, and mentally?
- Do I feel calm, neutral, or already overwhelmed and activated?
- Do I need to sleep, eat, or address any physical discomfort?
- Is my mind racing or present?
- Do I feel safe in my current environment?
- Do I have a way to regulate if something hard comes up?
- Am I in a private, quiet space where I can be fully present?
- Am I within my window of tolerance (p. 51)?
- What supports do I have in place if this becomes too much?
- What is my intention going into this exercise?
- Can I approach this with curiosity rather than pressure?

Best Practices and Safety Guidelines

To increase your chances of success while keeping safe, it's crucial to be honest with yourself about your current abilities and your tolerance level. This book isn't a substitute for personalized therapy with a licensed mental health professional and shouldn't be used as one.

Give yourself some breathing space after each exercise and consider setting aside time for rest and recovery. It's normal to feel more tired or tender after emotional work. When practicing a new skill, leave room for imperfection. Most things won't feel easy on the first try, and that's okay. Growth happens through repetition, not perfection.

Above all, let this process be one of compassion. Your healing doesn't need to be rushed. The most important thing is that you move at a pace that feels safe, grounded, and true to where you are.

Before You Begin

An important rule of thumb is to experience a baseline of safety and support before moving on to more emotionally intense work. Trauma recovery takes time, and moving too quickly can do more harm than good. I strongly recommend that you do not begin the trauma-focused exercises until you've developed the ability to stay within, or return to, your window of tolerance, defined on p. 51.

Exercises that directly engage with traumatic material will be marked with an ! symbol, signaling the need for caution. If you find yourself feeling overwhelmed, or out of control, it is best to skip these exercises or do them with the help of a trusted clinician. Before moving forward with any of these, take a moment to assess your current capacity and emotional regulation skills. If you notice . . .

- Frequent or intense dissociation
- Emotional flooding
- A rise in self-harming behaviors
- Suicidal thoughts or ideation
- An increase in panic attacks
- More frequent flashbacks
- A decline in basic functioning

. . . please discontinue self-guided trauma work and seek support from a licensed mental health professional. The purpose of these exercises is not to push you into extreme discomfort or to trigger painful memories. They are intended to help you mindfully cope with, process, and release pain—one small step at a time.

A GENTLE REMINDER

The healing process is rarely a straight line. You may experience a sense of progress one day and then a setback another day. That doesn't mean you're doing anything wrong. Try to approach these moments with grace, compassion, and curiosity; use them as opportunities to learn.

When things feel challenging, come back to the resourcing practices in Chapter 5 to establish safety and stability. If at any point you need extra support, do not hesitate to seek help from a professional. Healing is hard work, and you don't have to do it alone.

PART I

Understanding Complex PTSD

Chapter 1

Women and Complex PTSD

Change culture and you change lives. You can also change the course of history.

—RESMAA MENAKEM

IT'S A NATURAL AND IMPORTANT QUESTION: Why a book dedicated to cPTSD for women? While layered, the answer is also straightforward: Women, especially those from marginalized communities, are disproportionately affected by chronic, interpersonal, and systemic trauma. Research shows that women are twice as likely as men to develop PTSD (up to 12 percent of women experience the condition, compared to only 6 percent of men) with similar findings for emerging research on cPTSD.

Simply put, women are more likely to experience interpersonal and chronic forms of trauma—such as sexual assault and domestic violence—which are strongly linked to cPTSD. Before we can meaningfully support women on their cPTSD healing journey, it helps to take a closer look at why this may be.

If you're a woman reading this, you know it's no secret that from an early age, girls are taught how they "should" look, think, feel, and act. These cultural messages affect everyone, but for women, they often translate into harmful stereotypes that normalize or excuse their mistreatment. Gender-based violence—cognitive, emotional, physical, and financial—is a leading cause of trauma for women and girls. Yet supportive tools that honor how identity shapes trauma remain scarce.

Many existing resources on cPTSD focus primarily on childhood trauma. But for women, it's common for trauma to continue through adolescence and adulthood—during puberty when girls are sexualized, in romantic relationships, in the workplace, and in caregiving roles. For women of color, this vulnerability is compounded by systemic racism and hypersexualization.

Socialization along rigid gender binaries also shapes how trauma manifests. Women are taught to hide their pain, which often resurfaces later as shame, depression, dissociation, or hyperarousal. Men, by contrast, are taught to channel distress into anger, rage, or substance use. These patterns don't exist in isolation—they reinforce one another. When women are conditioned to suppress their pain and men are conditioned to externalize theirs, it creates a cycle that normalizes violence, silences women, and leaves both without healthy outlets for healing.

Gender is therefore central to the conversation around trauma. How you identify—and how others perceive you—shapes what happens to you, how you are treated, and what resources are available for you as you find your way out.

Your Pain Is Real

Historically, women's pain has been dismissed, minimized, or pathologized. The term *hysteria* was once a formal diagnosis, locating women's suffering in the uterus rather than in their lived experience. This led professionals to administer invasive, unnecessary procedures instead of addressing the true causes of the women's pain.

Similar patterns continue today. Women, especially women of color, are more likely to have their pain underestimated, undertreated, or attributed to psychological causes. Survivors are frequently labeled "dramatic" or "attention-seeking" and misdiagnosed with personality disorders, while their distress is overlooked.

This helps explain why many women hesitate to seek care and why their symptoms are misunderstood. It's also evidence that trauma-informed, culturally responsive care is both a moral imperative *and* the most effective means of treatment. Healing begins by affirming that your pain is real and legitimate, and that you are not "overactive," "broken," or "hysterical" for experiencing cPTSD symptoms.

While the systems around you may have denied or erased your pain, this book is here to assure you that your experience is real, your symptoms are normal responses to trauma, and healing is possible.

Trauma Is Layered

In most societies, women are expected to fulfill multiple roles—such as daughter, partner, mother, sister, friend, caretaker, and professional—while maintaining the appearance of being composed, available, and "happy to be there," even when they're struggling inside.

This emotional labor is invisible and exhausting, especially for women living with complex PTSD. Symptoms like emotion dysregulation, hypervigilance, dissociation, and brain fog frequently show up in relationships or work settings, yet are too often misread as weakness, instability, or incompetence. These misinterpretations can deepen shame, fuel an inner critic, and reinforce the fear of rejection—wounds already central to cPTSD.

On top of this, systemic inequalities intensify the load: The gender pay gap, inadequate maternity leave, limited childcare, and underrepresentation in leadership all shape women's daily reality. In professional spaces, assertiveness may be judged as aggression; in families, women often absorb the role of caregiver or peacekeeper; in healthcare (as discussed), symptoms are minimized or dismissed—especially for women of color.

The impact is magnified for marginalized communities, including women of color, queer and trans women, women with disabilities, and women experiencing poverty. Women in these categories disproportionately face violence, neglect, and exclusion, leading to higher rates of cPTSD and more severe symptoms.

The pressure to perform, cultural expectations, and systemic discrimination all weave into the lived experience of trauma for women. If you feel like you're carrying an invisible weight, you are not alone—you're responding to an unjust reality. Healing can feel like another full-time job; even the smallest step requires enormous strength.

As you begin reclaiming your voice, boundaries, and joy, expect resistance from systems that have benefited from your silence. Just remember this work isn't for them—it's for you.

Trauma Shapes Identity

Because complex trauma is often chronic, cPTSD can feel deeply woven into your identity. It influences how you move through the world, how you see yourself, and what you believe you're allowed to ask for.

Repeated trauma in formative relationships—especially in patriarchal or power-imbalanced settings like parent–child or romantic dynamics—can leave women feeling that their value lies in being palatable, pleasing, or useful to others. When this trauma begins in childhood, it can be especially difficult to separate your authentic self from the coping strategies you developed in order to survive. The parts of you that learned to perform, please, or stay small may begin to feel like your identity, rather than what you needed to do to stay safe.

In adolescence or adulthood, confidence erodes when you are minimized, sexualized, silenced, or betrayed by those you trust. You may internalize the belief that your worth is conditional—measured by how little space you take up, how productive you are, or how well you suppress your needs. This often leads to self-abandonment, people-pleasing, shame, and the belief that you are either "too much," "not enough," or fundamentally "broken." (As we'll cover later, you are none of these things.)

Women with cPTSD share common struggles such as emotional numbness, perfectionism, over-independence or codependence, and striving to keep others happy. Yet symptoms can look different from woman to woman, and even within the same person over time, shifting with circumstances like relationships, work, motherhood, or changes in safety.

One way to understand this is through the idea of "parts" of yourself that emerge in different situations. For example: a frightened child during conflict, a perfectionist at work, a part that numbs when emotions feel overwhelming, or a part that craves closeness but fears rejection. Each holds its own feelings, memories, and coping strategies. Depending on the moment, one part may take over to get you through. In cPTSD, vulnerable parts—such as the childlike, tender, or expressive aspects of you—are often pushed aside, while protective parts—like the perfectionist, caretaker, or "I don't need anything" persona—run the system.

Healing begins by recognizing which parts of yourself were abandoned for survival. It means re-parenting the inner child—or any version of yourself that needed care—rather than banishing her. It means making space for joy, curiosity, play, and desire, not only survival. While it can feel impossible to separate yourself from what happened to you, remember: You are not your trauma. You are a woman who survived an environment that did not honor her full humanity. The distance between your authentic self and your survival self may feel wide now, but with time and care, that gap can close.

An Underlying Truth

Perpetrators of abuse, as well as systems of oppression, benefit from keeping women feeling small, silenced, and stuck in cycles of shame. They rely on women to believe they are too weak or too broken to challenge the status quo. But recovery from cPTSD disrupts that narrative.

It reveals the truth that perpetrators try hard to distort: Women are not fragile—we are remarkably resilient physically, psychologically, and emotionally. Women have endured things we never should have had to, and yet we find ways to care for others, show up in the world, and keep moving forward. In healing, we choose not to let our pain define us. We say "no" to carrying the burdens of trauma forever.

Instead, we acknowledge we are intelligent, intuitive, and independent—capable of navigating even the most difficult challenges with confidence, compassion, and determination. With each step forward, you can unlearn the lies you were told about your worth and begin to live from a place of the fundamental knowledge that you were never too much. You were just around people who gave you too little.

Chapter 2

What Complex PTSD Is and Isn't

Trauma is not what happens to you.
Trauma is what happens inside you
as a result of what happens to you.

—GABOR MATÉ

THE AMERICAN PSYCHOLOGICAL ASSOCIATION (APA) defines trauma as "exposure to actual or threatened death, serious injury, or sexual violence." Yet in clinical practice, I see a much broader range of experiences that can trigger trauma responses—bullying or discrimination, neglect, witnessing a parent or sibling struggle with addiction, or living through an abusive relationship—to name just a few. Not everyone who experiences a traumatic event that meets the APA's criteria develops trauma-related symptoms. And many people whose experiences don't technically fit that definition still go on to suffer debilitating trauma responses.

This distinction matters. If we only define trauma as being caused by the most extreme events, we risk overlooking the very real wounds caused by experiences like neglect, bullying, or ongoing relational harm. For many women, these quieter but chronic forms of pain are exactly what give rise to cPTSD. Naming them as trauma is about validation. It affirms that your symptoms make sense, even if your experiences don't fit a narrow clinical checklist.

Complex PTSD, Defined

The term *complex trauma* refers to the events that happened—often chronic, relational, or developmentally disruptive. Complex PTSD is the experience of the long-term psychological and physiological effects that result from those events. Experiences that lead to complex PTSD include:

* Ongoing emotional, physical, or sexual abuse
* Domestic violence
* Childhood neglect or abuse
* Systemic oppression and discrimination
* Bullying
* Chronic illness and repeated medical trauma
* Severe mental illness in a close family member
* Exposure to emotional or psychological manipulation
* High-control religious environments
* Repeated foster care placement
* Institutionalization
* Human trafficking
* Incarceration
* Long-term caregiving in traumatic contexts

Since there is no single way to experience trauma, this book focuses less on where your pain originated and more on helping you understand and manage symptoms, find relief, and rebuild your sense of safety and empowerment.

From here, it becomes important to clarify how cPTSD differs from related conditions like PTSD and borderline personality disorder (BPD)—distinctions that matter both for accurate diagnosis and receiving adequate support.

Complex PTSD vs. PTSD

Technically speaking, to be diagnosed with PTSD, a person must experience or witness an event that was life-threatening, like serious injury, violence, or the threat of death. Complex PTSD, on the other hand, develops from the accumulation of many ongoing, relational, or non-life-threatening traumas—not one big event. This is the main difference between cPTSD and PTSD.

Both PTSD and cPTSD can reshape how you view yourself and the world around you. The difference is that cPTSD often develops slowly, over time, until the trauma feels woven into your very sense of self. With PTSD, people may still be able to see a clearer "before" and "after," whereas with cPTSD, the lines can blur—it can feel like the trauma became part of who you are.

The World Health Organization's (WHO) decision to recognize cPTSD as a formal diagnosis in 2019 marked an important step forward in the classification of cPTSD as its own experience. For survivors, this acknowledgment sent a powerful message: Your symptoms are real, distinct, and deserving of validation and care. For clinicians, it provided a clearer framework for treatment and research, helping ensure that people with cPTSD aren't misdiagnosed or given one-size-fits-all care designed for PTSD alone. While the American Psychiatric Association has not yet followed suit, the WHO's recognition reflects growing momentum in the mental health field and signals progress toward more accurate, compassionate support for survivors.

Complex PTSD vs. Borderline Personality Disorder

Many people searching for information on cPTSD are misdiagnosed or directed toward resources on borderline personality disorder (BPD). This happens because the two share overlapping symptoms, such as emotion dysregulation, feelings of emptiness, and unstable relationships. Both conditions are also linked to high rates of childhood adversity.

The difference is that while most people with BPD have a history of complex trauma, not everyone with complex trauma meets the criteria for BPD. This is why cPTSD needs to stand as its own diagnosis—to ensure survivors are properly validated and treated, rather than misdiagnosed or pathologized.

As we look at common cPTSD symptoms, remember these are natural survival strategies your mind and body developed in response to trauma. They may appear in everyday life or get triggered when no danger is present, but at their core, they began as ways to protect you.

When the Trauma Is What Didn't Happen

Unlike overt abuse, neglect is defined by what didn't happen: comfort that wasn't given, presence that wasn't consistent, needs that went unmet. Because it relies on absence rather than a clear event, survivors often struggle to validate their experience. Childhood neglect is one of the most common forms of complex trauma. It contributes to feelings of invisibility of the trauma itself and of the survivor's needs. Children are especially vulnerable, as their developing nervous systems rely on attunement and responsiveness to establish a sense of safety, secure attachment, and a strong identity.

Neglect teaches survivors that their needs are not worthy enough to receive attention, care, or protection. They often hear they are "too much" or "not enough." This develops into the belief that connection isn't safe or dependable, and that solo survival is the only way. As a result, neglect is closely linked to cPTSD symptoms such as self-doubt, shame, emotional disconnection, people-pleasing and fawning, and loneliness.

Like other forms of trauma, neglect leaves lasting imprints on the nervous system, attachment style, and sense of self. But healing is possible. Treatment for neglect often mirrors other trauma work, with an added emphasis on developing nurturing, reparative experiences that meet the needs that once went unmet. This approach teaches the nervous system what it feels like to be cared for, seen, and safe.

Complex PTSD Symptoms and Support

While this list of common cPTSD symptoms is organized into separate categories, they often overlap and influence one another. A psychological trigger can lead to a somatic reaction, which might then impact how you relate to others, and vice versa. For example, remembering a time you were harshly criticized can cause your body to tense and your stomach to knot. That physical discomfort might make you withdraw from a conversation with a friend or partner, creating distance in the relationship.

As you read through these definitions and symptoms, it's common to feel a profound sense of grief around what you didn't receive, or what was taken from you. It's important to honor that grief, and allow it as it passes through you, as we'll explore more in Exercise 30: Learning to Grieve.

If any (or many) of these symptoms resonate with you, please know you are not alone. These responses were once adaptive, developed to protect you during overwhelming or unsafe experiences. And because trauma responses are learned, they can also be unlearned. Despite the severity of symptoms, it is possible to find relief, rebuild trust in yourself and others, and feel more in control of your life.

PSYCHOLOGICAL SYMPTOMS

Intrusive memories or flashbacks

Nightmares and sleep disturbance

Hypervigilance

Paranoia and extreme mistrust

Negative self-beliefs ("I'm broken," "I'm too much," etc.)

Difficulty concentrating and brain fog

Identity confusion

Difficulty maintaining a coherent life narrative

Loss of core sense of self

Internal fragmentation (feeling like there are multiple "selves" inside you)

Suicidal ideation

Difficulty envisioning the future

Avoidance

Self-destructive behavior and impulsivity

Self-criticism and self-hate

EMOTIONAL SYMPTOMS

Emotional flashbacks

Chronic fear, anxiety, shame, and guilt

Panic attacks

Emotional dysregulation (intense mood swings or difficulty calming down)

Alexithymia (difficulty identifying and expressing emotion)

Chronic emptiness

Persistent sadness and grief

Irritability, rage, or explosive anger

Anhedonia (loss of interest in things that once brought joy)

Difficulty trusting positive feelings or experiences

Hopelessness and despair

PHYSICAL/SOMATIC SYMPTOMS

Chronic pain (e.g., migraines, fibromyalgia)

Gastrointestinal issues (IBS, nausea, bloating, appetite changes)

Fatigue and low energy

Tension and tightness in the body

Autoimmune flare-ups

Heart palpitations and shortness of breath

Hyperactive startle response

Difficulty falling or staying asleep, or hypersomnia (sleeping too much)

Hormonal imbalances

Frequent illness due to compromised immune function

Disordered eating patterns

Sexual dysfunction

RELATIONAL SYMPTOMS

Difficulty trusting others

Avoidance of relationships

Isolation

Fear of abandonment or rejection

Codependency and people-pleasing

Fear of intimacy and vulnerability

Overattachment or clinging in relationships

Difficulty setting or respecting boundaries

Conflict avoidance or excessive confrontation

Chronic relationship instability

Attracting or staying in unsafe/unhealthy relationships

Difficulty reading social cues or feeling "off" in social situations

Feeling fundamentally different or "other"

Loss of a stable sense of identity in relationships

Insecure attachment style

Suicidal Ideation

Suicidal ideation is a common symptom for complex trauma survivors. These thoughts can emerge when unprocessed trauma remains chronically activated. In that sense, suicidal ideation often functions as a protective response—a desperate attempt to shield you from further suffering, even if in extreme ways.

When suicidal ideation arises, it's crucial to meet it with self-compassion and curiosity rather than shame. It is usually not rooted in a desire to die, but in a deep yearning to end pain. Recognizing this can open the door to healing, guiding you toward longer-term trauma resolution.

If you are experiencing active suicidal thoughts, completing the Safety Plan in the Appendix can be a helpful step. Please also reach out for professional, trauma-informed support. For immediate help, call or text 988 (Suicide and Crisis Lifeline) or text 741741 (Crisis Text Line). With care and trauma-informed treatment, the core wounds driving these thoughts can be addressed, reduced in intensity, and, over time, even resolved.

Therapy and Medication

Finding a therapist can feel overwhelming. With so many providers, varying credentials, and modalities to choose from, it's natural to feel unsure about where to start. A helpful first step is exploring therapist directories where you can filter by specialty, modality, insurance, location, and personal preferences such as gender identity or cultural background. Once you've identified a few potential matches, consider scheduling a brief consultation—often around 15 minutes. This call can help you assess whether the therapist has experience with cPTSD, aligns with your preferred approaches, and feels like someone you could build a trusting relationship with over time.

While this book does not cover medication, many people with cPTSD also choose to work with psychiatrists or psychiatric nurse practitioners for additional support with emotional regulation. The decision to pursue medication is highly personal, and consulting with a trauma-informed prescriber can help you make a confident and compassionate choice.

Chapter 3

The Science Behind Complex PTSD

...Chronic stress affects the body in all kinds of ways, just as it does the mind. In fact, the mind and body cannot be separated.

—SUZETTE BOON

THE NERVOUS SYSTEM SPEAKS THE language of survival. When you encounter a threat, you must respond right now, immediately. When this response remains unresolved, the body may continue to mobilize as if danger is present, even when it's not.

Knowing this is powerful, because it means your reactions aren't signs of weakness or brokenness—they're your nervous system doing its best to keep you safe. When trauma remains unresolved, the body keeps sounding the alarm, even when no danger is present. Understanding this can help you approach your symptoms with more compassion and give you tools to gently teach your body the difference between past threat and present safety.

How the Stress Response Works

When you encounter a stressful experience, your brain triggers a cascade of signals that release stress hormones, such as cortisol and adrenaline. This is known as the hypothalamic-pituitary-adrenal (HPA) axis. These hormones mobilize your body to respond to the perceived threat by redirecting your energy toward survival functions. These include:

- **Fight**—anger, tension, irritability, sharpness
- **Flight**—restlessness, urgency, buzzing
- **Freeze**—stillness, flatness, numbness
- **Fawn**—people-pleasing, scanning for the needs of others

The autonomic nervous system drives these stress responses. It has two main branches: the sympathetic nervous system (SNS) and the parasympathetic nervous system (PNS). In a healthy stress response, once the threat passes, your body returns to its pre-emergency state.

Imagine yourself walking on the sidewalk, and you see a skateboarder ripping toward you. Your amygdala—the brain's fear center—alerts your SNS, which quickly mobilizes your body to jump out of the way to avoid danger. In theory, once your brain recognizes you are safe, your nervous system calms, slowing your heartbeat and restoring your body to a state of balance.

However, when the stressor is overwhelming, chronic, or inescapable, the body's stress cycle may remain incomplete. In these cases, the survival response can get "stuck," leaving the nervous system primed for danger even when no threat is present. Over time, repeated activation overwhelms the body's natural regulation system, keeping stress hormones elevated and the nervous system on high alert. This helps explain why present-day triggers can make you feel like the original trauma is happening again.

It's only natural, then, that psychological stress shows up in physical ways. Continuous activation has been linked to muscle tension, chronic pain, headaches, insomnia, high blood pressure, and digestive issues like irritable bowel syndrome. Researchers agree these are real, physical symptoms of unresolved stress and trauma. The mind and body are inseparable: What affects one invariably impacts the other.

Assessing Danger: The Brain

To understand more about why trauma responses persist, it helps to look at how specific parts of the brain process threat:

* **Amygdala:** Your brain's alarm system. It helps you process emotions—especially fear, danger, and other strong feelings. After trauma, the amygdala becomes hyperactive, priming you to interpret ordinary moments as threatening. This explains why someone with a history of physical abuse may have a strong stress reaction to even safe, affectionate touch.
* **Hippocampus:** The part of your brain that helps you remember things and provides context—like a mental filing system for your memories. Ongoing trauma floods the brain with stress hormones, wearing down—even shrinking—the hippocampus and interfering with its ability to encode memories. This is why you may vividly recall tiny or fragmented details, but struggle to piece together a complete narrative. In some cases, you might not remember the event at all. This is referred to as dissociative amnesia. It doesn't mean the trauma didn't happen—it's the brain's way of "forgetting" as a way to protect you.
* **Prefrontal cortex:** Normally in charge of reasoning, emotion regulation, and staying grounded, this part of the brain can go "offline" during traumatic stress. When that happens, the amygdala takes over, and the body responds as if the past trauma is happening now.

Together, a hyperactive amygdala, an impaired hippocampus, and a compromised prefrontal cortex drive many symptoms of post-traumatic stress. This is what underlies *emotional flashbacks*—intense feeling states that mirror the original trauma, often without clear visual memories. A small present-day trigger, like a partner's tone of voice, can ignite the body's old survival responses. In those moments, you end up swept into the emotional and somatic intensity of the past trauma, even if you cognitively know that you're safe. These responses are not overreactions—they are the body's learned survival mechanisms, trying to keep you safe, even when they are no longer adaptive.

REWIRING FOR SAFETY

Our brains are not fixed—they are constantly adapting in response to new experiences and learning. *Neuroplasticity* is the brain's ability to change, reorganize, and rewire itself by forming new neural connections throughout life. This means the changes trauma creates in the brain do not have to be permanent. Just as the brain learned patterns of survival and protection in response to trauma, it can also unlearn those patterns. Through healing experiences, it's possible to rewire the brain toward safety, connection, and regulation.

Seeking Safety: The Autonomic Nervous System

Your nervous system is constantly scanning your environment to determine whether you are safe or in danger. You may not even notice this process, because it operates below conscious awareness.

Here, we look at the autonomic nervous system (ANS), which regulates involuntary functions like heart rate, blood pressure, digestion, and arousal. It plays a central role in cPTSD because it influences how you process safety, threat, and recovery after stress. Its three branches include:

* **Sympathetic nervous system (SNS):** activates fight or flight
* **Parasympathetic nervous system (PNS):** supports rest and digest
* **Enteric nervous system (ENS):** manages digestion

A well-regulated ANS shifts smoothly between protection and calm. But when trauma is repeated or ongoing, this flexibility is lost. Stephen Porges's *polyvagal theory* explains how trauma disrupts the *vagus nerve*, a key part of the parasympathetic system.

One branch of the vagus nerve supports safety and connection; the other activates immobilization—freeze or collapse—when danger feels overwhelming. Here's a snapshot of what's going on inside, and why trauma responses can be so diverse:

* **Safety:** When your brain registers safety, the branch of the vagus nerve that supports calmness, connection, and presence is activated.
* **Threat (immediate):** When a threat is detected, the SNS kicks in to prepare for fight or flight.
* **Threat (inescapable):** If the danger feels overwhelming or inescapable, it can activate the other branch of the vagus nerve that leads you to numbness or collapse.
* **Blend:** Two blended responses can also occur, leading you to "freeze" and "fawn." This can manifest as high stress on the inside while appearing calm on the outside and may involve coping by seeking safety through compliant, people-pleasing behaviors.

These states are not inherently problematic—they are all adaptive responses designed to protect you. The challenge is when the nervous system becomes stuck in a state of survival, unable to shift between states of protection and safety. The brain misreads safety as threat, and body awareness may feel either overwhelming or muted.

Understanding trauma through this lens shifts the question from "What's wrong with me?" to "What did my body do to protect me?" This reframe can reduce shame and underscore the importance of body-based therapies, which work to strengthen vagal regulation and restore nervous system flexibility—helping you more accurately detect safety and embody connection.

Polyvagal Theory Chart of Trau

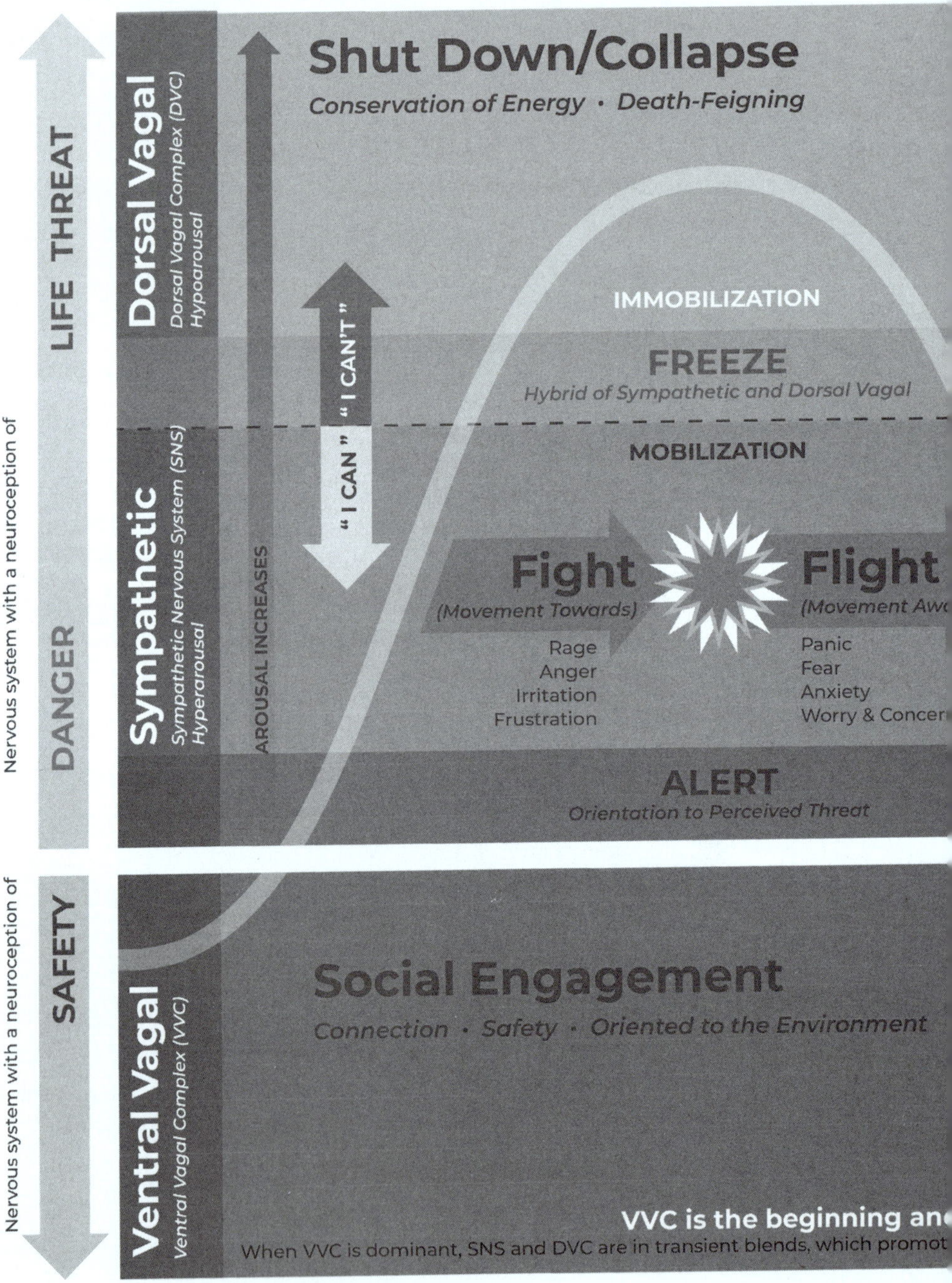

a Response

UPDATED 4/2025

Southwest Trauma Training
RUBY JO WALKER, LCSW

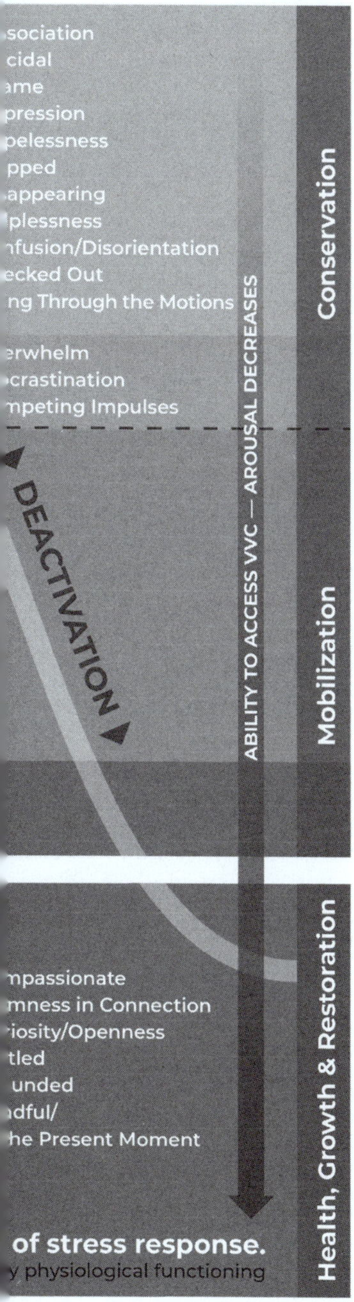

Parasympathetic Nervous System

Dorsal Vagal Complex (DVC)

▲ INCREASES

Fuel Storage and Insulin Activity
Immobilization Behavior (with fear)
Endorphins to Numb/Raise Pain Threshold
Conservation of Metabolic Resources

▼ DECREASES

Heart Rate · Blood Pressure
Temperature · Muscle Tone
Facial Expressions and Eye Contact
Depth of Breath · Social Behavior
Attunement to Human Voice
Sexual Responses · Immune Response

Sympathetic Nervous System *(SNS)*

▲ INCREASES

Blood Pressure · Heart Rate · Fuel Availability
Adrenaline · Oxygen Circulation to Vital Organs
Blood Clotting · Pupil Size · Dilation of Bronchi
Defensive Responses

▼ DECREASES

Fuel Storage · Insulin Activity
Digestion · Salivation · Relational Ability
Immune Response

Parasympathetic Nervous System

Ventral Vagal Complex (VVC)

▲ INCREASES

Digestion · Intestinal Motility
Resistance to Infection · Immune Response
Rest and Recuperation · Health and Vitality
Circulation to Non-Vital Organs (skin, extremities)
Oxytocin (neuromodulator involved in social bonds that allows immobility without fear)
Ability to Relate and Connect
Movement in Eyes and Head Turning
Prosody in Voice · Breath

▼ DECREASES

Defensive Responses

ker from Cheryl Sanders, Dr. Peter Levine, Anthony "Twig" Wheeler, and Dr. Stephen Porges

Chapter 4

Why an Integrative Approach Works

Safety is sensed, not believed.

—STEPHEN PORGES

TRADITIONAL TRAUMA TREATMENTS HAVE OFTEN centered on talk therapy, which relies heavily on the prefrontal cortex. But for anyone with a taxed stress response, this work is incredibly challenging until there is a felt—bodily—sense of safety and security. As a result, many people hit a plateau with strictly cognitive approaches. That's not to say cognition doesn't matter—far from it. Trauma shapes your thoughts, beliefs, and sense of self. A cognitive lens is essential for working with the inner critic, rebuilding self-trust, and integrating new beliefs. But it's rarely the whole story, and often not the first step.

Trauma is not a logical experience, it's emotional and embodied. The first step is to calm the nervous system—to signal safety within your body and present environment. From here, we continue to speak its language: sensation, movement, emotional processing, and memory reconsolidation. These methods calm the brain's alarm system, creating space for the logical part of the brain to come back online, and making it easier to sort through your experience and begin recovery.

Many traumatic experiences live in *implicit memory*—the kind stored in the body as sensations and emotions rather than as narrative or language. This is why recounting your trauma can feel unhelpful, or even retraumatizing. Experiential modalities such as Internal Family Systems (IFS), Eye Movement Desensitization and Reprocessing (EMDR), and Somatic Experiencing® target these implicit imprints, reaching parts of trauma that talking alone cannot.

This holistic lens is particularly impactful for women, because we are socialized to override our needs, disconnect from our bodies, and adopt roles of perfectionism, caregiving, or self-erasure. Much of traditional therapy was built on models by and for (usually white) men in power. An integrative approach makes room for the full spectrum of the human experience, including cultural, systemic, and relational trauma that may not be captured in conventional—and what many would now call biased—frameworks.

NOTE: When I say "spirit" throughout this text, I am not referring to religion, dogma, or any single belief system. This is about the deeper part of you that represents your aliveness, capacity for connection, purpose, intuition, and creativity. For some, the spirit may be shaped by faith. For others, it is grounded in nature, mindfulness, purpose, creativity, or community. Reconnecting with your spirit—however you define it—is a way of reclaiming wholeness within yourself. From there, it can also strengthen your connections with others and help you navigate the cultural and systemic wounds that may still live within.

Somatic Practices

We now know that allowing the body to complete its natural stress cycle is crucial for helping the nervous system return to balance rather than remaining stuck in survival mode. Somatic practices do exactly that.

Somatic-based approaches remind us that healing doesn't just happen through insight or reflection—it also occurs through a felt sense of safety, bodily awareness, and the rebuilding of inner and relational trust. The exercises in this book are designed to help you reconnect with your body, cultivate an embodied sense of safety, and gently release stored emotional energy.

Somatic Experiencing

Somatic Experiencing (SE), developed by trauma researcher and practitioner Peter Levine, helps individuals resolve unfinished stress responses by gently guiding them to notice and release tension or energy held in the body. Two core principles shape this practice:

* **Titration:** approaching traumatic material in small, manageable doses
* **Pendulation:** moving back and forth between dysregulation and regulation

These practices teach the nervous system how to handle stress more effectively, making it easier to process and recover from past trauma. For example, as you recall a difficult memory, you might notice your chest tightening, then shift awareness to the steady support of the chair beneath you. Moving between sensations in this way allows the body to naturally and gradually discharge stress—perhaps through a sigh, shake, yawn, or deep breath.

Nervous System Regulation

The goal of nervous system regulation is not to stay perpetually calm—that isn't realistic or even healthy—but to develop flexibility in how the nervous system responds. Many of the exercises in this book help tone the vagus nerve, a key branch of the parasympathetic system that supports safety, connection, and recovery.

Many are also polyvagal-informed, meaning they work by gradually reintroducing cues of safety, both individually and in relationships. For people with cPTSD, whose trauma often stems from relational harm, rebuilding the ability to feel safe in connection is a critical part of healing.

Moving, Breathing, and Other Somatic Pathways

Other somatic practices—such as breathwork, yoga, dance, and creative arts therapies—provide nonverbal outlets for accessing stored emotions and guiding the nervous system back toward balance.

These approaches have gained popularity for good reason: Research shows they can be especially effective for trauma survivors. Yoga and breathwork, for example, have been shown to reduce post-traumatic symptoms and improve emotional regulation, while dance and other creative movement therapies can promote regulation and foster resilience over time.

Internal Family Systems

Trauma-informed therapist Richard Schwartz developed Internal Family Systems (IFS), a compassionate model that recognizes how complex trauma creates extreme roles within our inner world. The idea is that we all have internal "parts" that take on different roles, as well as a calm, curious, compassionate *Self* that leads when parts are unblended. It's helpful to distinguish between *self*—our everyday sense of "me" that's often blended with our parts—and *Self*—our innate, centered awareness that relates to those parts with curiosity and care. Trauma disrupts this balance: Protective parts step in to ensure survival, and over time the system may be run by these protectors rather than the Self.

IFS is particularly supportive for cPTSD because it doesn't pathologize defenses or rush the healing process. Instead, it honors the protective role of each part. In IFS, every part—even the avoidant or painful ones—has a story and a purpose worth understanding. By working with these protectors, the system can eventually connect with exiled parts that carry deep pain, allowing them to release their burdens so the past no longer dominates the present.

IFS identifies three broad categories of parts:

* **Managers** work proactively to prevent pain.
* **Firefighters** reactively try to soothe or distract from pain once it's triggered.
* **Exiles** carry wounds of shame, fear, and unmet needs, often pushed out of awareness.

All your parts exist simultaneously, though only one takes the "driver's seat" at a time. For example, if sharing your interests as a child led to ridicule, that vulnerable part may become exiled. A people-pleasing manager might then step in to keep you safe, but if a similar wound is triggered later—say, being dismissed in a meeting—a firefighter may respond with emotional eating, dissociation, or self-harm to numb the pain.

IFS teaches that much of our suffering comes from conflicts among these parts and the disconnection from Self that results. Healing involves compassionately engaging with parts, understanding their roles and fears, and helping them release their burdens. When the Self leads with clarity and compassion, the system can move toward harmony—this is the primary goal of IFS therapy.

Research around IFS is promising: A 2021 pilot study found IFS effective in reducing symptoms among people with histories of multiple childhood traumas, and a more recent 16-week trial showed significant reductions in PTSD symptoms. While larger studies are still needed, findings suggest IFS is a flexible, client-centered modality well-suited for addressing complex trauma.

The IFS exercises in this book will help you get to know your parts, build trust with them, and understand what they need—so you can reconnect with your core Self, rather than feeling run by old survival strategies.

Eye Movement Desensitization and Reprocessing

Eye Movement Desensitization and Reprocessing (EMDR) is a therapy developed by researcher and psychologist Francine Shapiro. In EMDR, participants activate memories and then desensitize them using bilateral stimulation (BLS). This often involves following a therapist's fingers or a light bar with your eyes, but it can also include tapping, sounds, or gentle buzzers alternating from left to right. Bilateral stimulation helps the brain process memories differently, making them feel less overwhelming—more like past events rather than something happening in the present.

Researchers are still exploring exactly how EMDR works. One theory is that eye movements mimic what happens during REM sleep, when memories are consolidated. Another suggests that focusing on eye movements (or other bilateral stimulation) while recalling a distressing memory taxes the brain just enough to reduce the memory's emotional intensity.

EMDR follows a clear structure: beginning with building safety and grounding, then gradually guiding you through memories that still carry strong emotional charge. A full EMDR treatment plan addresses not only past trauma but also current triggers, strategies for managing them, and cultivating positive future experiences. EMDR is especially valuable for cPTSD because it doesn't require retelling every detail of what happened. Instead, it helps you process trauma on a body and emotional level first, then shifts to the cognitive effects by replacing harmful beliefs with more supportive ones, such as "I'm safe now" or "It wasn't my fault."

Although EMDR may sound intense, it is a highly adaptable approach. Skilled therapists pace the work carefully, ensuring you feel steady and supported before moving into deeper processing. Because EMDR cannot be self-administered, the EMDR-inspired exercises in this book focus on grounding and enhancing positive experiences through bilateral stimulation.

Dialectical Behavior Therapy

Dialectical Behavior Therapy (DBT), developed by psychologist, researcher, and author Marsha Linehan, is a present-focused, behavioral therapy. Its primary purpose is to help patients manage symptoms. Dr. Linehan originally developed this therapy to treat borderline personality disorder (BPD) and chronic suicidality, but today it also plays a valuable role in trauma-informed care because of the ways it teaches practical coping skills for the present.

The APA recommends a sequential approach to cPTSD treatment, and this is where DBT fits in. DBT teaches skills for managing strong emotional reactions, tolerating distress, and communicating effectively in relationships. These skills build self-efficacy and self-regulation, laying the groundwork for trauma processing.

DBT is structured around four treatment stages:

* **Stage 1: Behavioral Control**—focuses on reducing high-risk behaviors while establishing internal and external safety
* **Stage 2: Emotional Experiencing**—Begins deeper emotional work. In trauma-adapted DBT, this is where exposure to unprocessed trauma is introduced.
* **Stage 3: Ordinary Happiness and Unhappiness**—helps individuals set and pursue life goals while building self-respect
* **Stage 4: Capacity for Sustained Joy**—focuses on creating a life worth living through meaning and fulfillment

Within these stages are the four DBT modules that form the core therapeutic skills:

* **Mindfulness**—the foundation of DBT, which promotes present awareness and grounding
* **Interpersonal Effectiveness**—teaches how to assert needs, maintain self-respect, and build healthier relationships
* **Emotion Regulation**—helps individuals understand, assess, and manage emotional responses while maintaining self-validation
* **Distress Tolerance**—provides tools to endure life's inevitable pain and stress without resorting to self-destructive behaviors

The DBT-based exercises in this book are designed to help you manage overwhelming emotions, expand your ability to experience joy in the present, and create a life that feels fulfilling and aligned with what matters most to you.

Attachment-Based Therapy

Attachment-based therapy is an umbrella term for approaches grounded in the idea that early relational patterns shape how you relate to yourself and others. Because cPTSD often results from repeated relational trauma, attachment insecurity is one of its most pervasive impacts—making attachment-informed care an essential part of treatment. In fact, the APA's 2024 guidelines for cPTSD emphasize the importance of a relational approach. When trauma happens in a relationship, healing must also take place within the context of a safe and corrective relationship. This is where attachment-based therapies step in.

These therapies do not replace trauma-processing modalities such as EMDR or IFS, which directly address painful experiences. Instead, they serve as powerful complements, especially when trauma stems from pain or betrayal in relationships that should have been safe and secure. Many trauma therapists integrate relational approaches alongside modalities for memory processing. This dual method addresses both the emotional and interpersonal consequences of trauma, offering what many survivors never received: attunement, safety, and the experience of being deeply understood.

Relational Therapy

In relational therapy, the relationship itself is the intervention. The therapist models trust, attunement, boundaries, and co-regulation, which clients can gradually internalize and apply in their own lives. Research consistently shows that the strongest predictor of recovery is not the therapeutic model but the quality of the therapeutic relationship. For survivors of complex trauma, this matters profoundly—because learning how to be in safe relationships is the foundation for rewiring trust and connection. Relational practices will also be explored in Chapter 9, which focuses on building secure and supportive relationships.

Emotionally Focused Therapy

Emotionally Focused Therapy (EFT), originally developed for couples and later adapted for individuals, emphasizes attachment repair. Created by psychologist, researcher, and author Sue Johnson, EFT identifies patterns of disconnection while expanding emotional awareness. It helps clients express core needs and rework beliefs shaped by trauma. Like relational therapy, EFT focuses on emotional experiences rather than thoughts or behaviors, creating space for new, healing "corrective experiences" that can shift old trauma-based beliefs and support safer, deeper connections.

Narrative Therapy

Narrative therapy, developed by Michael White and David Epston—both social workers and therapists—is rooted in the idea that identity is shaped through the stories we tell about ourselves. With this model, writing itself is part of the healing—it keeps the prefrontal cortex engaged instead of letting the amygdala take over, allowing you to stay grounded in the present while processing the past. Research shows that writing about trauma brings measurable benefits, including improved immune function, fewer sick visits, fewer depressive symptoms, and greater emotional clarity. What's more, it offers a way to reclaim your voice, reshape identity, and restore meaning after trauma through expressive writing. For women whose stories have been distorted, silenced, or shaped by systems of harm, narrative therapy provides a gentle yet powerful path to self-authorship and emotional freedom.

Narrative therapy investigates internalized dominant narratives, asking you where your beliefs originated, who benefits from them, and how you might re-author your story. This makes it particularly well-suited for women with cPTSD, whose trauma often stems from repeated relational violations and oppressive societal systems. At its core, narrative therapy is an opportunity to step back into the role of narrator of your healing, rather than remaining a passive character in a story written by others.

Cognitive Processing Therapy

Cognitive Processing Therapy (CPT) emphasizes identifying and challenging the beliefs that emerge after trauma—often around safety, trust, control, and self-worth. Clinical psychologist, researcher, and professor Patricia Resick originally designed this structured, evidence-based approach to treat single-incident PTSD. Participants begin by writing an impact statement and then working to identify unhelpful or rigid beliefs that fuel shame, fear, or self-blame. With guidance, the clinician teaches participants how to challenge these beliefs and examine the evidence for them, reducing their power.

CPT can help clarify how trauma has shaped the way you see yourself, others, and the world. It supports the release of shame and self-blame and encourages more balanced and flexible thinking. Yet CPT has limitations, particularly for cPTSD. It does not directly address the chronic, developmental, and relational wounds at the heart of complex trauma. The model assumes a relatively regulated nervous system, which is often compromised in cPTSD. Because CPT leans heavily on cognition while neglecting the body and nervous system, some participants may find it invalidating—intellectually "aware" but emotionally unchanged.

In this book, some exercises draw from CPT's foundational tools, thoughtfully adapted for women with complex trauma. The goal is not to force your beliefs to become more "rational," but to gently explore which beliefs once protected you yet now keep you stuck. If you find yourself saying, "I know this logically, but I don't feel it," it may mean your system needs more regulation or trauma processing before new beliefs can truly take root.

This is why CPT is included last in this list. For many, healing begins with safety, somatic awareness, and acknowledgment of trauma. In trauma recovery, the prefrontal cortex comes back online *after* safety is established—not before. When the timing is right, CPT-based tools can be deeply effective in softening the inner critic and fostering a more compassionate, integrated view of self.

PART II
Exercises for Healing

Chapter 5

Establishing Safety and Emotional Regulation

The first task of recovery is to establish the survivor's safety. This task takes precedence over all others, for no other therapeutic work can succeed if safety has not been adequately secured.

—JUDITH HERMAN

THE EXERCISES IN THIS CHAPTER are designed to help you create a sense of internal and external safety. They focus on increasing mind-body awareness and strengthening emotional regulation. They are helpful for mild moments of disturbance and in moments of crisis.

Each of the practices here is rooted in *stabilization*—the ability to ground yourself and experience enough safety to engage with the events of your past without becoming overwhelmed, retraumatized, or turning to harmful coping mechanisms. Internally, stabilization tools help you recognize when you've been triggered, and then gently return to a state of regulation.

You can think of these skills like brakes. You don't want to wait until you're speeding downhill to test if they work. Use them regularly, and adjust them as needed. You can trust that you're building the foundation to be able to go deeper.

The Window of Tolerance

The window of tolerance (WOT) is a framework used to describe the zone where your nervous system feels steady enough for you to face hard material without feeling overwhelmed or checked out. A certain level of emotional response or experience is indeed necessary for processing trauma. However, if those emotions become too intense, it can push you beyond your comfort zone.

Signs you may be leaving your window of tolerance include:

* Heightened panic, anxiety, and overwhelm
* Dissociation, numbness, and shutting down

When either of these happen, it may mean you're moving too fast or too deep into traumatic material. Your nervous system becomes overwhelmed by too much emotion, sensation, or stress all at once. Therapists call this *flooding*. That's when your body and brain are overloaded with sensation or information. Your heart might race, your thoughts might get jumbled, or you might feel like you're drowning in emotion, unable to think clearly or calm down. This level of overwhelm can feel retraumatizing.

Trauma work starts with developing an awareness around your window of tolerance—when you've left it and how to bring yourself back. For those who have experienced ongoing trauma, the window of tolerance is often narrower. Many of the practices in this book are designed to help you widen your window through nervous system regulation. This allows for foundational trauma work, to eventually go deeper. In other words, you must be able to self-regulate before you start to unpack, analyze, and process your trauma.

There are multiple touchpoints throughout this book to help you assess your current stage in your window of tolerance. I encourage you to regularly check in with yourself, especially when trying any exercise marked with an **!** symbol that may involve activating material. Your safety and stability are the basis of trauma recovery. Especially when engaging in a self-guided process, becoming more familiar with and strengthening your window of tolerance allows you to—mindfully and methodically—dive in.

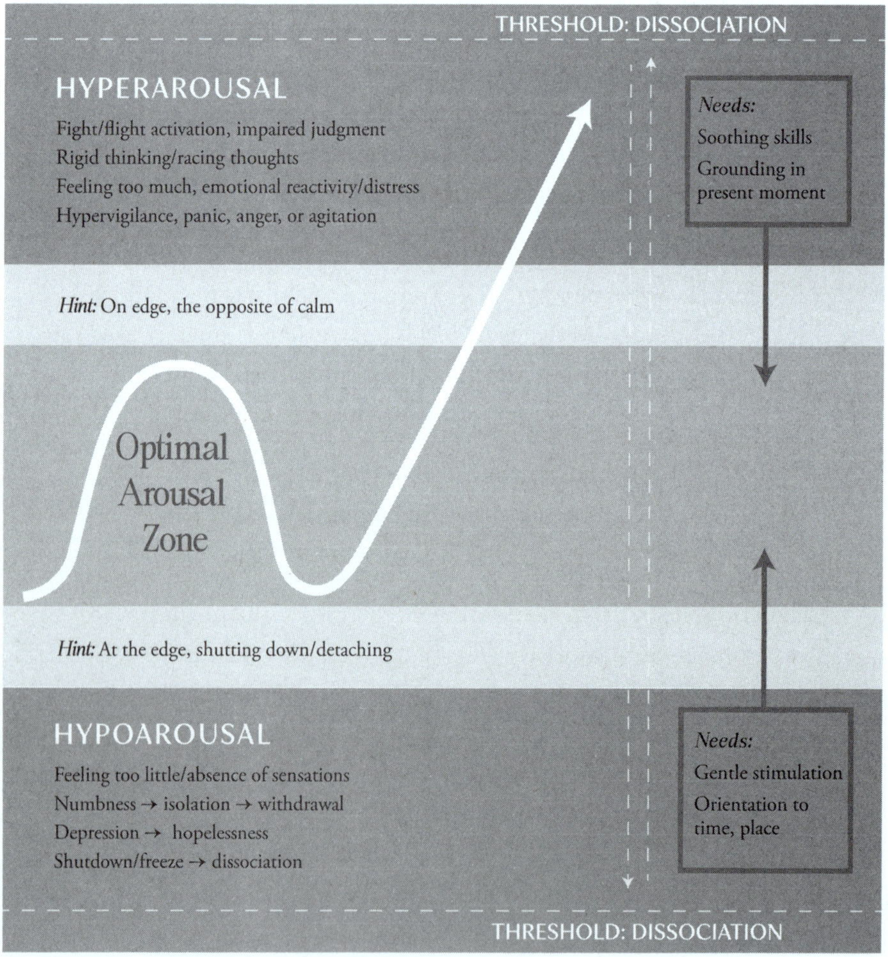

Adapted from "Understanding Your Window of Tolerance" by Mindfulness & Clinical Psychology Solutions

A Safe Place to Start

Stabilization also involves environment. In cases where it's not possible to escape, the goal is to create as much safety as possible within your current circumstances. This could involve building small moments of safety, such as focusing on your breath, grounding yourself through your senses, connecting with a trusted person, or setting small boundaries. It also means being realistic about what's possible in terms of healing while your trauma is ongoing.

Without environmental safety, trauma work is not possible. You may find yourself doing the emotional work of recovery, only to be retraumatized by ongoing harm. This can stall or even reverse progress.

If you are currently in an abusive or unsafe environment, you are not alone; please know it is not your fault. I strongly encourage you to seek out a setting that prioritizes your safety, as well as the safety of any dependents. While this can be incredibly difficult and may not be immediately feasible, it is a critical part of your healing journey.

Resources for Safety

Here are a few trusted resources that can help support you with safety planning, legal guidance, and shelter access:

* thehotline.org for safety planning, emotional support, and resources
* womenslaw.org for legal information and protection order guidance
* domesticshelters.org for a national directory of shelters and legal help

If at any point the material in this book feels overwhelming, triggering, or too difficult to process alone, please pause. There is no shame in stepping away to seek support. You deserve to feel safe, supported, and grounded as you move through this work. Healing does not have to be done in isolation.

! CLIENT STORY: BEGINNING FROM A SAFE PLACE

Sophia was in her late thirties when she came to therapy to address sexual trauma she experienced as an adolescent. During her intake, we discussed her previous therapy experiences. Sophia explained that a former therapist asked her to begin cognitive trauma processing in the second session. After the session, she noticed a resurgence in harmful thoughts. Sophia's therapist had asked her to share too much too quickly, before any window of tolerance had been established, along with any trust in the therapeutic relationship. Sophia's internal system worked hard to keep the details of her trauma out of her awareness. So, when she was prompted to revisit these wounds, a reactive part of her was triggered, attempting to cope with the pain of her trauma.

This case emphasizes the importance of stabilization before trauma processing. Once Sophia developed more awareness around her body's cues that she was leaving her window of tolerance, she could implement distress tolerance skills that led her to feel safer in her body. From here, we were able to establish a new, safe space to engage in deeper trauma therapy work.

EXERCISE 1

Identifying Your Window of Tolerance

WHAT YOU WILL NEED

Something to write with

A notebook or journal (optional)

TIME NEEDED

~10 minutes

This exercise will help you identify the edges for your window of tolerance (WOT), learning the early signs that you're exiting this window. Through this awareness, you can gently expand your window.

1. **Map each zone**
   - What do you feel physically, mentally, and emotionally when you're inside your window?
   - What does "too much" feel like?
   - What does "too little" feel like?

TOO MUCH

INSIDE MY WINDOW

TOO LITTLE

2. **Identify early warning signs**

   What lets you know you're about to leave your window? The things you notice might be subtle, like clenching your jaw, zoning out, experiencing racing thoughts, or becoming reactive.

   Try completing the following sentences:

   "My body's early signs of hyperarousal are . . ."

   ____

   "When I shut down, I tend to . . ."

   ____

3. **Learn how to get back to your window**

   WHEN YOU'RE ABOVE YOUR WINDOW (IN HYPERAROUSAL)

   Focus on gentle *grounding* that will help calm the nervous system. This can look like:

   - Deep breathing
   - Ice rolling on your face, neck, or wrists
   - Taking a cold shower
   - Grounding through your senses, e.g., eating sour candy or smelling essential oils

   WHEN YOU'RE BELOW YOUR WINDOW (IN HYPOAROUSAL)

   Focus on gentle *activation* that will help mobilize the nervous system. This can look like:

   - Rocking back and forth
   - Shaking your limbs
   - Running in place
   - Going for a walk
   - Focusing on sensations, e.g., the feeling of your seat beneath you or noticing your feet on the ground—bringing you back into your body

   We'll focus more on how to build out your regulation toolkit in Exercise 3.

EXERCISE 2

Befriending Your Nervous System

WHAT YOU WILL NEED

Something to write with

A notebook or journal

Colored pens or pencils (optional)

TIME

~15 minutes

This exercise uses the core principles in polyvagal theory to help you identify, track, and befriend your nervous system. It's about building awareness around how your body communicates with you—recognizing patterns and learning to gently regulate when you're stuck in a state that's not supportive.

1. **Review each state below**
   - SAFETY AND CONNECTION (VENTRAL VAGAL): In this state, you feel grounded, calm, and connected.
   - FIGHT OR FLIGHT (SYMPATHETIC): This state prepares you to respond to perceived danger. You might feel anxious, restless, angry, or overwhelmed.
   - SHUTDOWN (DORSAL VAGAL): This is the state of freeze, dissociation, or disconnection after a threat feels too overwhelming to face.

2. **Recall recent moments in each state**

   When did you feel grounded, connected, or at ease (ventral vagal)?

   ____

   ____

   When did you feel anxious, avoidant, or reactive (sympathetic)?

   ____

   ____

   When did you feel checked out, numb, or on autopilot (dorsal vagal)?

   ____

   ____

3. **Map your states**

On a blank page, draw two vertical lines to divide the page into three sections; label from left to right: Ventral, Sympathetic, and Dorsal.

Using the three recent moments you identified in Step 2, write down words that describe how that state feels for you. Use recent or old memories reminiscent of this state, and any images, symbols, or colors that capture the energy of that state.

By learning to identify where you are and how your nervous system communicates with you, you can begin to meet yourself with awareness and compassion, choosing tools that match your state rather than forcing yourself into one you're not ready for.

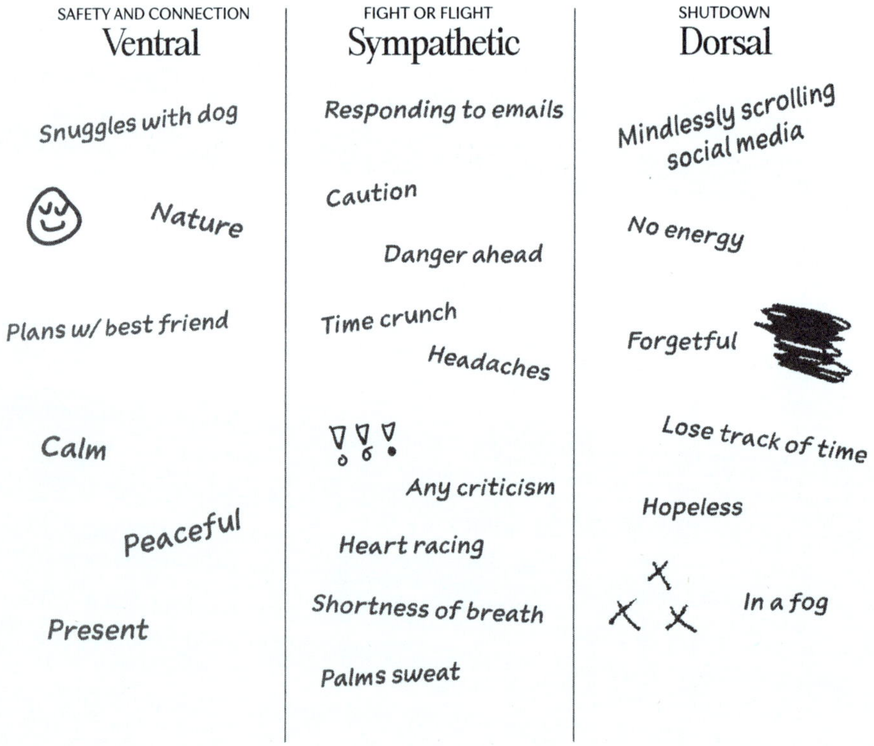

Adapted from Deb Dana's Polyvagal Interventions for Safety and Connection

EXERCISE 3

Building Your Grounding Toolkit

WHAT YOU WILL NEED

Something to write with

A notebook or journal

TIME NEEDED

~15 minutes initially, with ongoing practice

A well-rounded grounding toolkit includes physical, psychological, and social strategies that you can draw on when feeling over- or under-activated. Because hypoarousal (shutdown) and hyperarousal (overwhelm) require different interventions, it's essential to build two sets of tools: one to help you mobilize when you're under-activated and one to help you settle when you're over-activated.

1. **Consider what you need**
   Take a moment to assess if you are overwhelmed or shut down.
2. **Give yourself what you need**
   WHEN IT FEELS LIKE TOO MUCH (overwhelm), try tools that *ground,* soothe, and slow you. They might look like:
   - Massaging the sides of your neck (vagus nerve stimulation)
   - Humming, chanting, or singing
   - Taking a warm bath
   - Taking a cold shower (especially if panic feels sharp or destabilizing)
   - Giving yourself a hug (one arm under opposite armpit, other hand on opposite shoulder)
   - Doing slow bilateral butterfly taps (hands crossed on shoulders, tapping alternately)
   - Using a weighted blanket
   - Engaging in deep and slow diaphragmatic breathing (try 4-7-8 or box breathing)
   - Applying an ice roller on your face, neck, or wrists
   - Naming five things you can see, four things you can touch, three things you can hear, two things you can smell, one thing you can taste
   - Watching something light, funny, or familiar
   - Stepping outside and noticing what's around you

- Calling or texting a regulating, non-triggering person
- Resting in Child's Pose (p. 91) or another gentle yoga shape

WHEN IT FEELS LIKE TOO LITTLE (shutdown), try tools that *activate*, mobilize, and bring energy back into the body. They might look like:

- Doing jumping jacks, squats, or marching in place
- Shaking your limbs (start small, build intensity)
- Tapping your body lightly all over (start at feet and move up)
- Going for a brisk walk—bonus points for nature or sunlight
- Playing a sensory game: name all items in the room of a color of your choosing, something loud you can hear, something soft you can touch
- Engaging your sense of smell with a strong scent, such as coffee grounds
- Using sour candy, mint, lemon, or a fizzy drink to bring you back into your body
- Holding ice cubes in your hands (not extreme, just awakening)
- Listening to upbeat music
- Focusing on the sensation of your chair, a blanket, or something near you
- Opening a window or adjusting lighting to shift your environment
- Naming today's date, and then what's around you

3. **Test what works**
   Select a few tools to test out throughout the week. It's best to practice these before you need them. This will make them more accessible and effective when you're activated. When you've tried a tool, rank it from 0 (not helpful at all) to 10 (extremely helpful). You can grab a pen and write the number beside the bullets above or jot them down in a digital notebook. Swap out anything that feels ineffective or overwhelming.

EXERCISE 4

Collecting Your Self-Soothing Box

WHAT YOU WILL NEED

A container

Personal grounding items

TIME NEEDED

~15 minutes

For moments of shutdown or overwhelm, it can be helpful to have a physical self-soothing box—something to hold items that soothe you during moments of either shutdown or overwhelm.

1. **Choose a container**
   This could be a small box, pouch, or basket you can easily keep in a spot you'll reach for in challenging moments.
2. **Pick 4–6 items**
   These should be items that engage your senses and help you feel calm, safe, and grounded. *Examples: essential oils, a soft piece of fabric, mints, sour candy, a fidget toy, an affirmation card, a photo, a jade roller*
3. **Keep it accessible and practice**
   Keep your box somewhere easy to access when you notice early signs of distress. Practice using your items during low-stress moments so they become familiar when you need them most. A few go-to options are enough to help you return to center. This is meant to be a living toolkit that will grow with you.

EXERCISE 5

Noticing Your Glimmers

WHAT YOU WILL NEED

Something to write with

A notebook or journal

TIME NEEDED

~30 seconds, ongoing practice

Glimmers are the opposite of triggers; they're small cues of safety and connection. Noticing them helps rewire your nervous system toward regulation and calm.

1. **Look for signs**
   Track moments that spark warmth, openness, or a sense of calm. These are signs your body is experiencing safety.
2. **Name or record one glimmer a day**
   Examples: the way the sun shines through the trees, enjoying your favorite meal, seeing your pet after being away for the day
3. **Reflect on your glimmers**

   Do you notice any patterns around your glimmers?

   ____

   ____

   ____

   ____

   When do they tend to appear?

   ____

   ____

   ____

   ____

EXERCISE 6

Halting Your Flashbacks

WHAT YOU WILL NEED

Something to write with

A notebook or journal (optional)

TIME NEEDED

~3 minutes, with ongoing implementation

Trauma can make the present feel inaccessible, as if you're constantly reexperiencing painful moments from the past. *Flashback halting*, a process originally developed by Babette Rothschild, a leading trauma therapist known for bringing body awareness into the healing process, helps reorient you to the here and now.

Say the following sentences, filling in the blanks:

"Right now, I am feeling (*name emotion*) ____________

____

and I am sensing (*name bodily sensations*)

____

in my body, because I am remembering (*name the trauma—title only; no details*)

____________.

And, at the same time, I know that I am in the year (*name the year*)

____

currently at (*name where you are*)

____________,

and I can see (*describe your surroundings*) ____________

____________,

so I know (*name of trauma*)

____

is not happening now/anymore."

Developed by Rothschild, B. (2000)

EXERCISE 7

Redirecting Impulsive Reactions

WHAT YOU WILL NEED

A mindful moment

TIME NEEDED

~3 minutes

This exercise helps create a pause between a trigger and your response by helping you tune in to your body. Instead of reacting, you're choosing how to respond effectively. The STOP skill, adapted from the skills-based cognitive behavioral therapy DBT, is a simple but powerful tool for emotion regulation.

The acronym stands for:

- **S**top
- **T**ake a step back
- **O**bserve
- **P**roceed mindfully

Practice this skill with small, everyday triggers. The more you use it, the more likely it is to come naturally during bigger emotional moments.

1. **Stop: literally stop what you are doing**
   Freeze for a moment—no speaking, moving, or action. The goal is to interrupt the automatic reaction.
2. **Take a step back: breathe**
   Ground yourself. Create distance between the trigger and your next move.
   - This might mean taking a few breaths or stepping away. If you notice your emotions spiking, visualize turning an internal dial down to a more manageable level. Picture yourself as a thermostat, gently adjusting the temperature to help regulate the intensity.
   - These small shifts can help signal safety to your nervous system, making it easier to respond rather than react.

3. **Observe: notice what's happening inside and around you**
   What emotions are coming up? What are your thoughts saying? What are the facts of the situation—something an outside observer would also see? Observe without judgment.

4. **Proceed mindfully: choose how you want to respond**
   What is the most effective next step? What aligns with your values, your goals, and your long-term well-being? Proceed with an action that aligns with these values and long-term goals.

EXERCISE 8

Preparing for Challenges

WHAT YOU WILL NEED

A quiet space

Something to write with (optional)

A notebook or journal (optional)

TIME NEEDED

~15 minutes

Rehearsing how you will cope when you experience a trigger can help boost your sense of control and lessen anxiety about the unknown. This practice aims to make you feel more prepared and less overwhelmed when difficult moments occur. It also builds trust in your future self, reminding you that you have the tools to handle tough times. This can reinforce the belief that you are capable of managing what's ahead.

1. **Identify a future situation that might be difficult**

   Possible situation:

   ___

   ___

   Ask yourself, what specifically do I fear might happen? Is there a threat, or an anticipated catastrophe?

   ___

   ___

2. **Imagine the scenario in detail**
   Picture the event as vividly and realistically as you can. Include sensory details, like what you might see, hear, and feel. Let yourself walk through the experience step by step in your mind. If this starts to feel overwhelming, pause and use a grounding tool from your toolkit in Exercise 3. You can come back to this exercise whenever you feel ready.

3. **Rehearse how you want to respond**

Picture yourself navigating that situation in a way that utilizes your coping tools. This might include employing self-soothing techniques, setting boundaries, practicing assertiveness, or using positive self-talk.

If you struggle to come up with an answer, think of a person, real or imagined, who embodies a quality or resource that can help you handle the triggering situation. Visualize that person responding in a way that aligns with your needs and values. As you envision them easing distress and resolving the issue, imagine yourself in their position.

What does a response that reflects your values and tools look like?

4. **Reflect and repeat**

Write down how it felt to rehearse it. This helps to solidify the imagery and integrate your emotional experience. You can also note any parts that felt too difficult to engage with and revisit them gently at another time. Rehearse as many times as you need to build confidence in handling this trigger.

EXERCISE 9

Strengthening Your Capacity for Joy

WHAT YOU WILL NEED

Something to write with

A notebook or journal (optional)

TIME NEEDED

~1 hour per day

Experiencing joy is both grounding and healing. Feeling joyful enhances your capacity to access positive memories—a necessary skill when working through painful ones. Getting more comfortable with joy (as a concept and experience) also fosters more compassionate and hopeful beliefs about yourself.

1. **Make time for pleasant activities**

   Schedule a daily pleasant activity for the coming week. The more detailed and accessible your plan is, the more likely you are to follow through. But also, avoid scheduling activities that feel out of reach or unrealistic. Start small and build from there.

2. **Rate its effectiveness**

   Once you complete the activity, rate (0–10) how mindful you were during the activity, and how pleasant (0–10) it was for you.

   To rate the MINDFULNESS, ask yourself, "Was I fully present, noticing my thoughts, feelings, and surroundings without judgment?" A score of 0 means you were distracted entirely or on autopilot; a score of 10 means you were fully engaged and in the moment.

   To rate PLEASANTNESS, consider how enjoyable, satisfying, or comforting the experience felt. A score of 0 means not pleasant at all, while a 10 means it was as enjoyable as you can imagine.

Day of the Week	Pleasant Activity (who, what, when, where)	Mindfulness During Activity (0–10)	Pleasantness of Experience (0–10)

Adapted from Linehan (2014) DBT Skills Training Manual

EXERCISE 10

Creating Internal Ease

WHAT YOU WILL NEED

A quiet place with minimal interruptions

Something to write with

A notebook or journal (optional)

TIME NEEDED

~10 minutes

This is a visualization exercise commonly used in EMDR therapy that helps you create an internal sense of safety and ease. It serves as a grounding resource you can return to during or after difficult moments to regulate your nervous system and restore a sense of safety and stability.

1. **Think about a safe space**
   Identify a place or a state of being, real or imagined, where you feel calm, safe, or at ease. This can be somewhere in nature, a special room or nook in your home, or someplace completely imagined. This can also be a state of being, such as after a yoga flow, meditation, or following an accomplishment.

2. **Focus on the sensory details**
   Allow yourself to fully step into the place, immersing yourself in the experience.
   - What do you see?
   - What do you hear?
   - Any smells?
   - What body sensations?
   - What emotions do you notice when you are in this place?

3. **Establish a cue word**
   What is a word or short phrase you associate with this place?

4. **Add bilateral stimulation**

   Bring up the immersive experience, linking it with your cue word or phrase, while adding slow back-and-forth/bilateral taps. You can cross your arms and tap your shoulders or tap your knees for as long as it feels positive.

NOTE: If your recurring trauma happened in childhood, repeat this exercise to develop a safe/calm state for your inner child. If you choose to do this, add a real or imagined kind and responsible adult who can look over and care for your inner child (children need supervision!). Oftentimes, people may have difficulty with the resource figure because part of the trauma is that there was no safe adult. This is where imagined people or real-life individuals come into play—Ted Lasso, Nina Simone, Mister Rogers, and Michelle Obama are some people that my clients have imagined. Real figures can include therapists, community leaders, teachers, or clergy. Regularly activating your calm state, even after minor stressors, can strengthen your ability to handle intense moments. The more you practice, the more accessible it becomes when you genuinely need it.

EXERCISE 11

Picturing a Safe Container

WHAT YOU WILL NEED

A quiet environment with minimal interruptions

TIME NEEDED

~5 minutes

The "container" is another visualization exercise often used in EMDR therapy. It allows you to compartmentalize distressing material in a healthy manner, so you can return to it when you feel more resourced and supported. This tool can help reduce distress between trauma processing sessions or during moments of emotional flooding. Use this exercise whenever something feels too big to hold all at once.

1. **Settle into the moment**
   Take a few grounding breaths and settle into the present.

2. **Imagine your container as something sturdy and secure**
   Picture your container as able to hold anything you need it to. It could be a vault, a locked chest, or anything that feels strong and private to you that only you can open.

3. **Fill your container**
   Bring to mind any thoughts, emotions, or memories that would be unhelpful or overwhelming to face at this time. This can be anything that would pull you out of your window of tolerance or make it harder to focus on daily life. Visualize them filling your container. Take as long as you need to fill your container.

4. **Seal your container**
   Once everything is inside, visualize closing and sealing your container. Imagine locking it and placing it somewhere safe in your mind. This could be a closet, a basement, or maybe a therapist's office. Somewhere you know you can access it, but where it won't intrude on its own.

EXERCISE 12

Meeting Your Needs

WHAT YOU WILL NEED

A quiet space

Something to write with (optional)

A notebook or journal (optional)

TIME NEEDED

~30 minutes for reflection, with ongoing work if needed

Trauma work requires space. Without enough emotional energy or stability, the experience might cause re-traumatization or worsen symptoms. This exercise uses a trauma-informed needs hierarchy to help you check on areas that may need more focus. It specifically concentrates on two basic types of needs: physiological needs and safety needs.

Remember, you don't need to have everything "figured out" before beginning trauma work. That said, the more stable your system is, the more capacity you'll have to do the deeper healing work safely and sustainably.

1. **Self-check**
   Where are you now? Rate each area below from 1–5
   (1 = unmet, 5 = stable)
   - **Physiological needs:** access to food, water, shelter, clothing, sleep, and treatment for physical illness
   - **Safety needs:** personal security, such as your body being physically safe (not living in a currently abusive or neglectful environment)
   - **Physical security:** employment, financial stability, or access to resources

2. **Create a supportive action plan**
   If you notice gaps in your foundational needs, consider how you might address them, without judgment. This might involve:
   - Prioritizing consistent meals and rest
   - Reaching out for financial or housing support
   - Seeking community resources

Chapter 6

Deepening Body Awareness

The body of the traumatized individual refuses to be ignored.

—BABETTE ROTHSCHILD

THIS CHAPTER BUILDS ON THE stabilization techniques practiced in Chapter 5 with practices rooted in Somatic Experiencing and Sensorimotor Psychotherapy. These exercises each focus on restoring the body's natural rhythm by gradually releasing stored survival energy and replacing it with a felt sense of internal safety.

Together, they help you develop a stronger mind-body connection, accessing your body's inherent wisdom and feeling deeply connected to the present moment. As always, if any of these exercises feel too triggering, allow yourself to pause and seek support.

! CLIENT STORY: BUILDING SAFETY IN INTIMACY

After several years of working together, Lauren, a 28-year-old client, had made meaningful progress in managing her depression. As we prepared for trauma processing, we turned toward the lasting effects of sexual trauma she endured in college—most notably, the dissociation she continued to experience during sex with her supportive partner. Because her body still reacted as if intimacy were unsafe, our work centered on helping her gently reconnect with her body as a whole. This included nervous system regulation strategies and gradual exposure to body-based experiences.

We used *pendulation*, a somatic technique that involves shifting between sensations of discomfort and neutrality, which helped her remain within her window of tolerance. Over time, this also included intentional, non-sexual self-touch to build safety and presence. Alongside EMDR, which targeted some of her specific traumatic memories, these somatic tools allowed Lauren to slowly reinhabit the body she had long disconnected from. As her nervous system began to trust the present moment and orient to safety, she became increasingly able to stay grounded during intimacy.

! EXERCISE 13

Tolerating Discomfort

WHAT YOU WILL NEED

A quiet space

TIME NEEDED

~15 minutes

Pendulation is a Somatic Experiencing technique developed by Peter Levine, a psychotherapist and the founder of the modality. It helps you build your capacity to stay with intense or uncomfortable sensations, without becoming overwhelmed.

The idea is to notice discomfort in the body, and then gently shift your attention back and forth between that sensation and one that feels neutral, pleasant, or more tolerable. This technique allows your nervous system to experience that it can move in and out of difficult states safely. With practice, pendulation can expand your ability to be with discomfort without being consumed by it.

> **Tuning In**
> Check in with yourself and your window of tolerance. Is this a good time to gently explore sensation?

1. **Settle in and notice**
   Begin by sitting or lying down in a comfortable position. Let your body settle in. Notice your breath, the weight of your body, and the feeling of being supported by the surface beneath you. Let yourself orient to safety in your current space.

2. **Find a place of discomfort**
   Gently focus on a sensation in your body that feels uncomfortable but tolerable. This might be a tightness in your chest, a clenching in your stomach, or a heavy feeling in your limbs. Add descriptors to the sensation: Is it hot, cold, tight, sharp, dull, moving, still, heavy, or light? Stay with this awareness for a few breaths.

3. **Find a place of neutrality or ease**

   Now shift your attention to a different area of your body that feels neutral, less charged, or even pleasant. Parts of the body that feel quiet, steady, or areas that feel looser, softer—your skin, hands, toes. Let yourself rest your attention there. Similarly, qualify this sensation, and stay with that sensation for a few breaths.

4. **Pendulate**

   Begin gently moving your awareness back and forth from the place of discomfort to the place of neutrality or ease for a few seconds each. Repeat this 3–5 times. Do not try to change the sensations. Instead, show your system that it can move in and out of discomfort.

5. **Return to neutrality**

   Return to a neutral place in your body. Notice how you feel, and if anything shifted or softened.

EXERCISE 14

Releasing Trapped Energy

WHAT YOU WILL NEED

A quiet and private space

A blanket or cushion for comfort

When bodies can't complete a fight-or-flight response during a traumatic event, that stress response can become stuck. Over time, it can lead to nervous system dysregulation, chronic tension, emotional overwhelm, and other physical symptoms. This often manifests as hypervigilance, shutdown, or being easily triggered. Reconnecting with your body allows you to process the past, improve your ability to handle current stress, and reduce reactivity to triggers.

This exercise, adapted from Somatic Experiencing, is about noticing what your body wants to do and following that impulse gently. This process works best in small doses and can be repeated as many times as needed.

> ### Tuning In
> Check in with your body. Does it feel like it can tolerate sitting with distressing material? Bring in any regulation tools you've identified that can help you should you find yourself outside your window of tolerance.

1. **Choose a starting point**
   Scan your body and notice if there's any tightness, tension, or unusual sensation. Another option is to bring up a mild to moderately distressing event and notice your body sensations associated with it.

2. **Notice the impulse**
   Ask yourself, "If my body could do anything right now, what would it want to do?" Let your body guide you without judgment. You may feel an urge to:
   - Shake out your hands
   - Stretch your jaw
   - Push your feet into the ground

- Kick
- Push
- Rock back and forth
- Curl up
- Make fists
- Throw punches

3. **Complete the impulse**
   Let yourself complete these urges slowly and curiously. Trust small impulses, as they may be the beginning of releasing trapped energy.
4. **Allow for release**
   As you move, notice if your body begins to release energy naturally. This may look or feel like shaking or trembling, heat or coolness, yawning or sighing, or tingling or softening. Let it unfold naturally.
5. **Integrate**
   Come back to stillness and feel your body supported by the surface beneath you. What do you notice now? Has anything softened, shifted, or become more present? You might feel more grounded, or more tired.

EXERCISE 15

Embodying Your Inner Warrior

WHAT YOU WILL NEED

A private space

A yoga mat or a comfortable floor space

TIME NEEDED

~20 minutes

After trauma, the body commonly becomes a site of fear, disconnection, or shutdown. This exercise invites you to reconnect with your body as a vessel of strength, grounding, and power. Warrior poses in yoga were traditionally designed to cultivate courage and focus. We use them in trauma work because the poses are a symbol of reconnecting with your inner strength.

Tuning In

Body-based practices can feel especially vulnerable. Before you begin, check in with how you feel in your body today. Do you notice any tightness, tension, or unusual sensation that may need your attention before you proceed? Is there any part of your body that feels neutral or at ease?

1. **Start with grounding (Mountain Pose)**
    - Stand with your feet hip-width apart. Press down through your feet.
    - Feel the earth holding you up.
    - Let your arms rest by your sides.

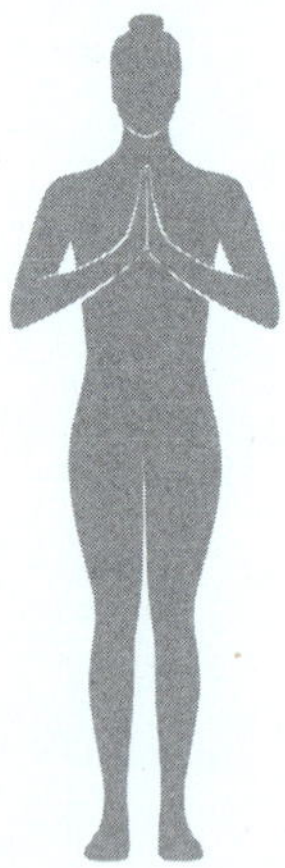

2. **Move into Warrior II**
    - Step one foot back, arms extended out to the sides, front knee bent.
    - Gaze over your front hand. Imagine strength radiating from your center through your fingertips.
    - Hold for 2–3 breaths.

3. **Transition to Reverse Warrior**
    - From Warrior II, tilt your front arm up and back, hand reaching to the sky. This is a gesture of rising and reaching.
    - Notice the sensations of taking up space, and of growing.
    - Hold for 2–3 breaths.

4. **Return to stillness**
    - Let your body rest in Child's Pose (p. 91) or a seated position, inviting your muscles to soften.
    - Notice the shift between movements of power and rest.

■ EXERCISE 16

Noticing, Not Reacting

WHAT YOU WILL NEED

A quiet space

Something to write with (optional)

A notebook or journal (optional)

TIME NEEDED

~15 minutes

The SIBAM model outlines five channels through which we process and integrate our experiences:

Sensation: raw, physical experience in the body

Image: mental pictures, metaphors, or dreamlike visuals

Behavior: movements, impulses, postures

Affect: emotions and feelings

Meaning: interpretation, story, or belief

By slowing down and exploring each of these elements, we create more space to notice rather than react, and to integrate rather than suppress. This exercise can be used after a triggering moment, in response to mild activation, or to simply build body-based awareness. You can jot down the responses in a journal, or make mental notes.

1. **Choose a starting point**
   Think of a recent situation that brought up some mild to moderate discomfort, such as feeling a bit anxious, frustrated, or irritated. Begin with an experience that feels manageable to work with.

2. **Gently explore the SIBAM channels**
    - SENSATION: Tune in to your body and ask, "What am I feeling physically right now?" Are there areas of tension, heat, coolness, buzzing, or numbing? Where do you feel this most?
    - IMAGE: Notice any symbols, colors, or mental pictures that come up.
    - BEHAVIOR: Do you want to curl up, stand tall, shake something off, or walk away? What is your posture like right now?
    - AFFECT: Name the emotion or mood you're feeling, and where you can locate that feeling in your body.
    - MEANING: What story or belief is emerging from this moment? Is it about you, others, or the world?

3. **Integrate and reflect**

    Take a breath and look over what you noticed.
    - Did anything surprise you?
    - Were some channels easier to access than others?
    - What happens when you witness all of these pieces together, instead of just one?

EXERCISE 17

Embodying the Self

WHAT YOU WILL NEED

Something to write with

A notebook or journal (optional)

TIME NEEDED

~20–30 minutes

How you move, speak, make choices, and interact with the world shapes how you experience yourself. Healing deepens when it moves from something you *think about* to something you *embody*. This means engaging with life in ways that reflect your truest, most integrated Self.

This exercise is designed to help you recognize what it feels like to be led by your Self—the part of you that is calm, creative, compassionate, confident, curious, courageous, connected, and clear—and to anchor that awareness in your body. The more familiar you become with these sensations, the easier it becomes to notice when you're aligned and to return there when you're not.

In learning to identify your body's cues of safety and alignment, you'll begin shifting from reactivity to choice, from surviving to living with intention. This exercise helps you practice that connection so you can navigate daily challenges from a grounded, embodied place.

1. **Recall a Self-led moment**
   Think of a time when you felt any of the following qualities, even if it was brief:
   - Compassion
   - Creativity
   - Connection
   - Confidence
   - Calm
   - Clarity
   - Courage
   - Curiosity

2. **Bring the Self-led moment to mind in detail**
   Where were you? How did your body feel? What were you thinking?

3. **Notice your body cues**
   Take note of your posture, breathing, and any physical sensations. Are your shoulders back? Is your breath deep and steady? Are your muscles relaxed?
   Write down the cues you notice.

   ____

   ____

4. **Visualize Self-energy in a difficult moment**
   Now picture a situation in the near future that might feel stressful or triggering. Imagine yourself moving through it from this same true sense of Self. See if you can hold your body cues, whatever they may be, from the prior step. This can look like speaking calmly or making decisions from a place of clarity. See yourself completing the interaction while still connected to the Self.

5. **Reflect**
   Every time you embody your Self, especially in difficult moments, you're rewiring your system to trust that grounded, compassionate leadership is possible.

   One way I can bring my Self into the moment is ______________

   ____

   ______________________________.

! EXERCISE 18

Bypassing the Thinking Brain

WHAT YOU WILL NEED

A private space with room to move

A timer (optional)

Something to write with

Art materials of your choice

TIME NEEDED

~40 minutes

Modalities like movement and art bypass the thinking brain, giving the body a chance to express itself through gesture. This exercise invites you to track sensation, move in response to it, and express it visually. It's about expression—you do not have to be a dancer or an artist to participate. Repeat this practice as often as you'd like, especially when you feel stuck in sensation and can't find the words.

> **Tuning In**
> This practice can stir up emotion. Evaluate your emotional bandwidth, check in with your window of tolerance, and bring any grounding tools that are effective for you.

1. **Attune to your body**

   Start by standing or sitting comfortably.

   - What are you feeling in your body right now?

   ____

   ____

   ____

   ____

   - Is there an area that feels heavy, tight, buzzing, numb, or unsettled?

   ____

   ____

   ____

   ____

- Place a hand over that area if it feels supportive.

2. **Let the body move**
    - Set a timer for 5–10 minutes (or go without a timer).
    - Ask yourself: If this sensation had a movement, what would it be, and how would it move?
    - Let your body respond to the sensation with spontaneous movement. This could look like rocking, swaying, curling in, shaking your hands or arms, or stretching—allow the movement to be messy and intuitive.
3. **Transfer it to art**
   When you're ready to transition from this movement, take out your art materials.
    - What shape, color, or image matches what you just felt?
    - Let yourself creatively express the feeling.
4. **Reflect**
   What does this art evoke in you? How do you feel looking at it? Did anything shift in your body from when you started?

■ EXERCISE 19

Exploring Self-Touch

WHAT YOU WILL NEED

A quiet, private space

Something to write with

Blanket or lotion (optional)

TIME NEEDED

~10 minutes

Reconnecting with your body is about gradually rebuilding safety, trust, and choice. One way to do this is through intentional and safe self-touch. It can activate the body's parasympathetic nervous system, and certain techniques have shown that touch patterns can reduce stress hormones, soothe the amygdala (your brain's alarm system), and help integrate dysregulated emotional states.

Most importantly, when you choose how and where to touch your body, you can begin restoring the agency that trauma may have disrupted.

Tuning In

This exercise can be particularly triggering for those with body-based trauma. Remember to check in with your window of tolerance, to start and build this exercise slowly, and to pause at any point.

1. **Settle in**
   Sit or lie down in a supported position. Gently bring your attention inward. How connected do you feel to your body right now? Are there any areas that feel more neutral or safe to touch?

2. **Offer gentle, safe touch**
   Start with whichever one of these options feels most comfortable to you:
   - HAVENING-STYLE TOUCH: Cross your arms lightly over your chest. With your palms or forearms, gently stroke from shoulders to elbows, alternating sides. Repeat in a slow, rhythmic motion for a few minutes.
   - STILL TOUCH: Place a hand gently over your heart, belly, or another safe-feeling area. Let it rest. Feel the warmth of the contact. Focus softly on the grounding sensation.

- **GENTLE HOLD**: Cradle your face, or hold the back of your neck or thighs, as if you are offering comfort to yourself.

3. **Pause and reflect**
   Has anything softened or shifted? Do you feel more present, or more distant? Did anything feel soothing or surprising?

! EXERCISE 20

Stretching-Feeling Internal Body Signals

WHAT YOU WILL NEED

A space to move

A yoga mat (optional)

A quiet place to sit

TIME NEEDED

~10 minutes

Stretching activates the parasympathetic nervous system—downregulating sympathetic activation, reducing cortisol levels, and improving vagal tone. When practiced regularly, stretching can help relieve stored tension and become a ritual of somatic regulation.

Stretching can also stimulate *interoception*, or your ability to feel internal body signals. For trauma survivors, improving interoception is key to restoring body awareness. If you have any injuries, chronic pain, or lack mobility, please consult with your doctor on potential modifications for this exercise.

> **Tuning In**
> Stretching can activate emotional releases, especially for those with body-based trauma. Check in with your window of tolerance and ensure you have grounding tools nearby if you choose to proceed with this exercise.

1. **Choose any (or all) of the suggested stretches below**

SEATED FORWARD FOLD (HAMSTRING + BACK BODY RELEASE)

This position lengthens the vagus nerve and helps quiet the fight-or-flight response. To begin:

- Sit on your mat with your legs extended in front of you.
- Inhale to lengthen your spine, then exhale and gently fold forward from your hips, letting your hands rest on your thighs, shins, or feet (whatever is accessible).
- Soften your knees.
- Hold for 5–8 slow breaths, letting your head and shoulders relax.
- (optional) You can add a mantra or an intention, such as, "I'm safe to let go."

SUPPORTED CHILD'S POSE (LOW BACK + HIP RELEASE)

Child's Pose activates pressure receptors along the front body and spine, calming the nervous system and reducing blood pressure.

- Come onto your hands and knees, bring your big toes together, and widen your knees.
- Extend your arms out in front of you.
- Sit back toward your heels and rest your forehead on your mat.
- Breathe slowly for 5–8 breaths, letting your belly expand with each inhale.

CHEST OPENER (FRONT BODY + HEART SPACE RELEASE)

Many trauma responses involve collapsing inward. This stretch invites openness and counteracts protective postures that signal danger to the brain.

- Sit or stand tall, interlacing your fingers behind your back (or grab opposite elbows if your shoulders are tight).
- Inhale and gently pull your hands down and away, lifting your heart and opening the chest.
- Hold for 5–8 breaths, keeping your jaw and shoulders relaxed.

2. **Aftercare—notice what arises in your body**
   After stretching, notice any sensations in your body. Did anything shift, physically, emotionally, or energetically?

EXERCISE 21

Creating a Movement Menu

WHAT YOU WILL NEED

Something to write with

A notebook or journal

TIME NEEDED

~20 minutes, with ongoing implementation

Regular movement improves heart rate variability (HRV). This is a key marker of nervous system flexibility—the ability for your nervous system to move between states in response to your environment.

The goal of this exercise is to help you find forms of movement that are grounding, enjoyable, and sustainable to help increase your HRV and regulate your nervous system after trauma.

1. **Reflect on your movement history**
   - What types of movement or exercise did you enjoy as a kid?
   - Are there any types of movement that felt safe, or joyful?
   - Are there any types of movement you associate with shame, punishment, or performance?
   - What types of movement help you feel more in your body, instead of in your head?
   - Do certain types of movement help you sleep better, reduce anxiety, or help you feel more connected to yourself?

2. **Create your movement menu**

   Make a list of 6–8 movement activities that feel doable. These can be accessible in the moment, such as stretching, or more structured, like swimming or jogging. Write down anything that sounds even a little bit appealing or that has felt good in the past. You can use the following categories to help spark ideas:
   - RHYTHMIC: walking, cycling, rowing, rebounding, elliptical machine
   - EXPRESSIVE: dance, martial arts, yoga flow
   - GROUNDING: stretching, tai chi
   - INTENSIVE: weightlifting, HIIT, sprinting
   - PLAYFUL: roller skating, hula hooping, trampoline, aerial yoga
   - NATURE-BASED: gardening, trail walking, kayaking

3. **Choose a low-barrier option**

   Identify 2–3 items from your list that feel most accessible to you. Pick one of those and schedule it for sometime this week. Start small—the goal is to begin activating your system.

4. **Reflect**

   Immediately after the activity, take some time to reflect on the experience.
   - How did your body feel before you moved?
   - How did it feel during?
   - How do you feel now, emotionally and physically?
   - What did you notice about your breath, posture, or tension levels?
   - Would you want to do this again? Why or why not?

5. **Build your personalized movement plan**

   As you experiment with different types of movement, you'll begin to learn which ones help you regulate. Build a go-to list of trauma-informed movement practices that work for you. It can feel extra supportive to create specific options for different emotional states, for example:
   - When I'm anxious, I can . . .
   - When I feel flat or numb, I can . . .
   - When I feel angry, I can . . .

EXERCISE 22

Developing Your Somatic Story

WHAT YOU WILL NEED

A quiet space

Something to write with

A notebook or journal (optional)

TIME NEEDED

~15 minutes, with ongoing practice

When your nervous system shifts into a state of fight, flight, freeze, fawn, or shutdown, your brain naturally begins to craft a narrative that matches that state. This exercise, inspired by Deb Dana's work around polyvagal theory, helps you track your physical sensations (and, thereby, your nervous system state), observe the corresponding story, and then separate the two. In practicing this type of somatic awareness, you can begin to respond rather than react to stressful situations or memories.

1. **Tune in to the sensation**

   Close your eyes or soften your gaze to turn your attention inward. Bring awareness to your body.
   - What sensations are most noticeable?
   - Is there tension, pressure, shakiness, or numbness?
   - Is your breath shallow or deep?
   - What's the energy in your limbs? Fidgety, heavy, or still?

2. **Stay present with the sensation**

   Without trying to interpret or fix anything, just notice. Stay here for 2–3 minutes, if it feels tolerable.

3. **Name the state**

   Gently inquire, "What state might I be in?" Use the categories of fight, flight, freeze, fawn, and grounded.

4. **Let the story emerge**
   Now ask, "What story does this state want to tell me?" Let your mind wander freely. Without censoring, complete the following sentences:

   - Right now, I believe ______________________________.
   - Other people are ______________________________.
   - The world is ______________________________.
   - The future looks ______________________________.
   - Do these thoughts match how your body feels? ______________________________

     ____

5. **Be with this awareness**
   Instead of shifting your state, see if you can stay with the awareness of its presence right now.

6. **Reflect**
   Ask yourself, "If I were in a different state, how might this story change? Have I noticed this pattern before?"

Chapter 7

Gently Processing

Unprocessed memories are generally the basis of negative responses, attitudes, and behaviors. Processed memories, on the other hand, are the basis of adaptive positive responses, attitudes, and behaviors.

—FRANCINE SHAPIRO

NOW THAT YOU'VE BUILT BASIC tools for self-regulation, the next step is to gently process the experiences that still live in your mind and body. This phase is often one of the most challenging because it requires facing pain that your system has successfully avoided.

The exercises in this chapter will help you work with your system as you revisit painful memories, adapt unhelpful trauma-based stories, and reduce the power of triggers that pull you back to the past.

Before proceeding with the following exercises, take a moment to check in with yourself by completing the following prompts:

If I notice myself becoming overwhelmed or emotionally activated, I will

____.

Examples: grab a cooling pack or ice roller, go for a walk

If I notice myself shutting down or feeling numb, I will

____.

Examples: press my hands firmly against the wall, do jumping jacks, eat sour candy

Take a moment to consider the ways you are far more resourced now than you were during the period of your trauma. Consider each of the following:

* What relationships or resources do you have now that you didn't have before?
* What personal strengths have you built in your adult life?
* In what ways is your life safer now, or more hopeful?

REMEMBER: Slow trauma processing is safe trauma processing. Listen to your system's limits. If at any point you feel destabilized, disconnected from reality, or overwhelmed beyond what feels manageable, please stop. These are signs that your system is trying to protect you from going too far, too fast. If you notice symptoms worsening, if you're dissociating frequently, or if you're unable to stay within your window of tolerance, it is essential to seek support from a licensed trauma therapist.

! CLIENT STORY: AN EXPERIENTIAL "DO-OVER"

Isabelle began therapy hoping to understand how growing up with a narcissistic father shaped her fear of rejection and contributed to her entering a series of similarly harmful relationships in adolescence. She tended to lose herself in relationships, both personally and professionally. For Isabelle, trauma processing involved several layers: mapping out protective and wounded parts of herself, gently revisiting emotionally charged memories with increased support, and creating corrective experiences. I like to call these experiential "do-overs"—a way to meet needs that went unmet in childhood.

By addressing both past wounds and present patterns, Isabelle began to break free from familiar relational dynamics—strengthening her sense of identity and reducing the emotional charge around feedback and perceived rejection. With a clearer internal compass, she found herself more willing to take risks, pursue meaningful opportunities, and build relationships from a place of authenticity rather than fear or familiarity. Isabelle's story illustrates how trauma healing isn't about erasing the past, but about learning to leave it there in order to move forward in a way that feels self-led and fulfilling.

! EXERCISE 23

Uncovering Unprocessed Pain

WHAT YOU WILL NEED

A quiet space

Something to write with

A notebook or journal

TIME NEEDED

~20 minutes

By gently observing present-day emotional triggers and tracking physical sensations, you may begin to uncover past experiences that shaped your current responses. In doing so, you can start to connect the dots between past and present. The memories and experiences you identify can then serve as guides to uncover and better understand your unprocessed pain.

> **Tuning In**
>
> Check in with your window of tolerance before proceeding with this exercise. If you're feeling numb, flooded, or disconnected from your body, pause here. This exercise is not recommended if you are currently struggling with dissociation or intense dysregulation.

1. **Identify present triggers**

   Identify 2–3 recent moments where you felt emotionally triggered. From those, choose the *least* intense example to start with to ensure your nervous system stays within a tolerable range. (You can revisit more emotionally charged moments once you feel more confident with the exercise.)

2. **Scan your body**

   Bring yourself back to that triggering moment as vividly as feels tolerable:

   - Gently scan your body from head to toe.
   - What emotions and physical sensations occur? Examples of sensations might include tightness in your chest, a lump in your throat, heaviness in your limbs, a racing heartbeat, tension in your jaw, or temperature changes.
   - Stay with the sensations and observe without judgment.

3. **! Bridge to earlier experiences**

   Let your attention rest on the sensations you are feeling:

   - Without trying to force anything, ask yourself: when is the earliest time I remember feeling this same sensation or emotion in my body?
   - Trust whatever comes to mind—an image, a feeling, a flash, or even a vague sense.
   - If you start to feel overwhelmed, bring your attention back to your surroundings: open your eyes, move your body, or name a few things you can see to orient to the present.

4. **Identify (and jot down) what arises**

   If a memory, image, or moment surfaces, gently notice and record:

   - What emotions are present
   - Any beliefs you associate with the moment
   - Any sensations still active in your body

If you find yourself feeling numb, disconnected, or like nothing is coming up, your system may be protecting you through dissociation. That's okay. This is a typical and adaptive response to overwhelming material. In these cases, it can be beneficial to seek support from a trauma therapist who has experience working with parts of the self/ego states.

! EXERCISE 24

Identifying Your Parts

WHAT YOU WILL NEED

A quiet space

Something to write with

A notebook or journal (optional)

TIME NEEDED

~30 minutes

Building a compassionate relationship with each of your parts is an essential step in the trauma healing process. If you remain unaware of these parts, they can take over when you face perceived threats, emotional overwhelm, or vulnerability. This exercise is about understanding the different aspects of your internal world: your wounded parts, your protective parts, and your current adult Self.

> **! Tuning In**
>
> This exercise can activate dissociative tendencies or disorders. If you experience feeling numb, outside of your body, or like you're in a dream, please proceed with an abundance of caution or under the guidance of a professional.

1. **Enter a calm state**
   Take a few deep breaths to settle into your current space.

2. **Recognize your parts**
   Bring to mind your managers, firefighters, and exiles (summarized below). Remember, these are broad categories for the various parts of you.
   - MANAGERS work proactively to prevent pain.
   - FIREFIGHTERS reactively try to soothe or distract from pain once it's triggered.
   - EXILES carry wounds of shame, fear, and unmet needs, often pushed out of awareness.

3. **Dig deeper into your parts**

   Check the ones you recognize as showing up within you. You can also add your own.

   - ☐ The hard-working part
   - ☐ The part who people-pleases to avoid conflict
   - ☐ The part who plans, keeps lists and schedules, and keeps you organized
   - ☐ The critical part who points out flaws, so you don't get hurt by others
   - ☐ The little girl who feels vulnerable and wants to be held
   - ☐ The lonely one who craves belonging
   - ☐ The part who carries shame and hides because of past mistakes
   - ☐ The scared child who flinches when voices get loud
   - ☐ The performing part who always smiles and pretends everything's fine
   - ☐ The fixing part who rushes to solve everyone else's problems
   - ☐ The perfectionistic part who won't let you rest until you get it just right
   - ☐ The rageful part who lashes out to protect softer parts
   - ☐ The skeptical part who questions motives and avoids trust
   - ☐ The controlling part who tries to keep everything safe and predictable
   - ☐ The guard who keeps people at a distance
   - ☐ The part who escapes, avoids, procrastinates, and distracts
   - ☐ The impulsive part who uses substances, food, sex, or work to cope
   - ☐ The numbing part who dissociates and spaces you out
   - ☐ ____________________

4. **Envision your adult Self taking your place in a meeting room**

   Find just the right place for you, as you are today, and let yourself settle in.

5. **Invite all of your parts into the room**

   Invite all the various parts of yourself to enter the room and take their places around a table. Watch as they come in. If they can't come to the table, maybe they stay in the periphery, or they stay in an adjoining room—notice who and what you see. These can be as concrete or abstract as you see them.

6. **Reflect**

   After completing the visualization, take some time to reflect, and complete the table to help you keep track of who and what you saw.

Identify part	Does it have a name?	Age?	What is its function?	Who are its allies? Who is it in opposition with?	Is it oriented to the present, or does it think it's in the past/ future?	Does it have any stories it would like to share with you?

Adapted from Fraser (1991)

EXERCISE 25

Thanking Your Parts

WHAT YOU WILL NEED

A quiet space without interruptions

Something to write with (optional)

A notebook or journal (optional)

TIME NEEDED

~10 minutes

After we become more familiar with our protective parts (see Exercise 24, p. 101), an important step is to thank them. The truth is that every part of us is trying to protect us in some way, even if its actions seem misguided or disruptive. The more we ignore or reject these parts, the louder and more persistent they tend to become. Yet when we approach them with curiosity and compassion, we reduce internal conflict. Over time, this helps soften our relationship with the aspects of ourselves we tend to judge the most.

1. **Settle in and identify the target part**
    - Get comfortable in your space. Feel the support of your seat, take a few deep breaths, and notice what's happening in your body.
    - What part of you is asking for attention: protective instinct, coping behavior, inner critic?
    - Let one part come into focus. Note that this exercise can be repeated as often as needed with different protective parts.

2. **Befriend the target part**

    Bring this part to your awareness.
    - Where do you feel it in or around your body? Is there an image, color, or age associated with it?
    - How do you feel toward it right now? It's important to approach this question with curiosity or compassion. If you notice anger, judgment, or shame, *pause*. Approaching this exercise from a critical stance can reinforce the negative self-talk it aims to alleviate.
    - How did it get its job? What does it want you to know? Is there anything it's afraid will happen if it doesn't work so hard to protect you?

3. **Thank the part**

   Let it know it's been seen and appreciated.

   - If it's protecting a younger version of you, gently show it where you are now. Tell it that you have more tools today, and that it doesn't have to work so hard or alone.
   - Ask if there's anything it needs to feel safe letting go or stepping back. Remind this part that you're simply trying to unburden it from carrying so much.
   - Offer final words of gratitude or compassion that feel right.

! EXERCISE 26

Bringing Kindness to Core Wounds

WHAT YOU WILL NEED

Something to write with

A notebook or journal

A quiet space

TIME NEEDED

~30–60 minutes

In this exercise, you'll begin connecting current protective patterns and defense mechanisms to the core wound they're associated with. The aim of this step is to bring kindness toward the mechanisms you created to protect yourself.

Tuning In

Where are you in your window of tolerance? Do you have the capacity to connect with some painful life experiences at this moment? Do you have your regulation tools for when you're overwhelmed or when you're shutting down?

1. **Make a list of your top four protective patterns**
   These might include behaviors such as:
   - People-pleasing
   - Overworking
   - Perfectionism
   - Avoidance

2. **Rank these patterns from the ones you notice most often to least often**
   Place a number (1–4) beside each protective pattern.

3. **Identify your starting point**
   Start with the pattern you ranked as least present. This makes it easier for your system to explore it without becoming overwhelmed. Begin with the sentence, "I [insert pattern] because . . ."

   EXAMPLE:

   I people-please because I feel uncomfortable when others are upset.

4. **Work your way downward**

   Continue the sentence several times, each time expanding on your previous statement by answering with another "because . . ." See where the answers take you. Keep going until you reach a point where your answer feels like a concrete fact about your history or circumstances.

   EXAMPLE:

   I people-please because I feel uncomfortable when others are upset.

   I feel uncomfortable when others are upset because I worry they'll withdraw or leave.

   I worry they'll withdraw or leave because I fear being alone.

   I fear being alone because it makes me feel unlovable.

   It makes me feel unlovable because I learned that love had to be earned. (This is the natural end in this example.)

5. **Recall life circumstances**

   Once you've identified the origin point, gently reflect in your notebook.

   How old were you when you first remember feeling or learning this?

   What was happening in your life at the time?

   What were you trying to protect yourself from?

6. **Piece it together**

   You are beginning to reform your trauma narrative—a compassionate, curious look at the "why" behind your patterns. In your notebook, write out the following, and fill in the blanks.

   My protective pattern that is not currently serving me is ______________

   ____.

The emotion I tend to feel right before using this pattern is ________________

____

____.

The subconscious belief driving it is ______________________________________

____

____.

I learned this around age ___________________________, during a time when

____

____

____

____.

7. **Repeat**
   Repeat this with the other protective patterns you've identified.

8. **Reflect and return to the present**
   Notice any shifts in your ability to offer compassion to these patterns now that you better understand their origins. If it feels right, you might:
   - Thank the pattern for how it once tried to protect you.
   - Place a hand on your heart or offer another comforting gesture.
   - Use a gentle phrase such as, "You were doing your best with what you knew at the time."

9. **Ground yourself (again) in the present moment**
   Feel your feet on the floor, notice your breath, or look around and name a few things you can see or hear, to remind yourself that you are safe in the present moment.

! EXERCISE 27

Breaking Unsupportive Cycles

WHAT YOU WILL NEED

Something to write with

A notebook or journal

TIME NEEDED

~20 minutes

While unhealthy behaviors, like substance use, isolating, or lashing out, may offer short-term relief, they almost always come at a cost to yourself and the people around you. Over time, they can reinforce shame, keep you stuck in a cycle of avoidance, and contribute to long-term emotional distress.

Part of processing underlying trauma involves identifying and beginning to shift these patterns so you can move toward healthier, more sustainable ways of coping.

> **Tuning In**
> This exercise involves assessing and reflecting on unhealthy patterns of behavior. Please ensure you feel grounded before proceeding and pause any time throughout the exercise.

1. **Identify your cycle of behavior**
    - What are the warning signs? These are physical sensations, emotions, thoughts, and behaviors that happen before you have difficulty managing impulses.
    - What is the last straw? In other words, what is the event that breaks your ability to maintain your emotional control and triggers giving in to the urge?
    - What exactly is the unhelpful behavior?
    - What are the short-term results? (Maybe you experience relief.)
    - What are the long-term results? (Maybe it reactivates the cycle.)

2. **Identify a safety plan at each point in the cycle**
    What could you do as a safety plan at:
    - The early warning signs (usually before increased risk signs)
    - The increased risk signs (usually before the last straw)
    - The signs of emergency (after the last straw and before the behavior)

3. **Develop a healthy coping card**

Use the information from Step 1 to help you fill out the prompts below:

Triggering situation (can be any situation, physical sensation, emotion, thought, behavior): ____________________

____

How you used to respond: ____________________

____

Safe and healthy ways to help yourself: ____________________

____

Results of responding in the old, unsafe and unhealthy way: ____________________

____

Short-term results: ____________________

____

Long-term results: ____________________

____

Results of responding in the new, healthy way: ____________________

____

Short-term results: ____________________

Long-term results: ____________________

! EXERCISE 28

Viewing Your Memories as an Adult

WHAT YOU WILL NEED

A quiet space

Something to write with (optional)

A notebook or journal (optional)

A memory that feels mildly to moderately distressing as identified in the earlier exercises

TIME NEEDED

~25 minutes

Compassionate memory viewing allows you to gently begin processing trauma from a safe distance, approaching your experiences with curiosity and care rather than overwhelm.

This exercise invites you to gently reflect on a trauma-related memory through the eyes of your grounded, adult Self. Here, you'll acknowledge its emotional imprint and begin to reshape the meaning it holds.

Tuning In

Before you begin, check in with yourself. Are you feeling grounded enough to reflect on a difficult memory without feeling overwhelmed, numb, or flooded? Are you leading from your adult Self, as opposed to a childlike or reactive part?

CAUTION: This exercise can activate multiple traumatic experiences. If other memories begin interfering with this exercise, return to your container (Exercise 11, p. 72). If the container does not help to move the other memories aside or you are out of your window of tolerance, discontinue this exercise.

Start with the least distressing memory and work your way up only as your system feels ready.

1. **Recall the memory from a distance**
   Imagine you're in a calm, safe room with a screen in front of you. On the screen, the memory you've chosen to explore is playing. It's important to remember that you are not inside the screen. You are an observer. You can press Pause at any time. As you look at the screen, observe:
   - What is happening in the scene?
   - What do you notice about your prior self's emotions, body posture, or voice—as they were happening in this moment?

- Is anything preventing you from moving forward, playing over and over again, or standing out?

2. **Invite in your present-day Self**
   Now, picture your grounded, present-day Self entering the room where the memory is playing.
   - What does your present-day Self understand now that your prior self couldn't have known?
   - How might your present-day Self want to care for or protect this previous version of you?

3. **Offer a message from your present-day Self**
   From the perspective of your present Self, write or say a short message to your past self.
   - What do you want her to know?
   - What was never her fault?
   - What strengths did she show, even if she couldn't see them then?

4. **Notice any protective parts**
   As you try to connect with your prior self, do any protective parts arise? Is there a shaming voice? A resistant or skeptical voice rejecting compassion? If so, pause and ask:
   - What is this part trying to protect me from?
   - What is good or helpful about its presence?
   - What would feel threatening about letting my younger self receive compassion?

5. **Offer empathy to your parts**
   Notice if that shifts anything in how you feel toward your younger self.

6. **Check in with yourself and repeat as necessary**
   Return to this practice with other memories, repeating as many times as feels supportive.

! EXERCISE 29

Experiencing a Do-Over

WHAT YOU WILL NEED

A quiet space

Something to write with

A notebook or journal (optional)

A memory where your needs went unmet, where the stress response feels incomplete, or where you think you're lacking closure

TIME NEEDED

~15–20 minutes

Trauma therapy allows you to imagine an outcome where your needs were met, where you were protected, or where you were able to respond appropriately to what was happening. While we can't change the past, the nervous system reacts powerfully to imagery associated with symbolic repair.

> **Tuning In**
>
> Am I grounded enough to revisit this memory through imagination, without becoming overwhelmed? Do I feel like my adult, present-day Self is online?

1. **! Recall the memory**
   Choose a memory where you felt powerless, abandoned, or ashamed, but avoid your most overwhelming experience. Briefly recall what happened, focusing only as much as feels tolerable.

2. **Imagine what you need**
   Now, picture the moment unfolding differently:
   - Who steps in to comfort or protect you?
   - Or, what if you, as your grounded, present-day Self, entered the scene to take action?
   - What would it look like to fight back or complete the stress cycle? What words would you say?

3. **Allow your power to grow**
   Picture yourself growing larger while the perpetrator shrinks, calling in an army for protection, standing your ground with strength, or simply rewriting the years with a nurturing figure by your side.

4. **Embody that support**
   How does it feel in your body to have power, choice, or support? Let your nervous system fully step into the experience of being believed, protected, or empowered.

5. **Anchor the experience**
   Write a few lines about what happened in your do-over scene.

   - What shifted in your body?

     ____

     ____

     ____

   - What shifted in your emotional experience?

     ____

     ____

     ____

   - What felt different this time?

     ____

     ____

     ____

EXERCISE 30

Learning to Grieve

WHAT YOU WILL NEED

A quiet space

Something to write with

A notebook or journal

TIME NEEDED

~15–20 minutes

Grief is a felt experience. By allowing yourself to make space for it, you're honoring the part of you that needed more. Here, you'll begin to accept and release what was lacking from your past. The exercise works on processing lingering pain while acknowledging what you went through and the losses you experienced as a result.

> **Tuning In**
>
> Before proceeding, check in with your body and emotional state. Can you be with sadness, anger, or longing without becoming too overwhelmed?

1. **Name the loss**
   Reflect on one thing your past self needed but didn't receive. *Examples: protection, being believed, unconditional love, a safe adult, or a voice that said, "This wasn't your fault."*

2. **Let the grief speak**
   Give your grief a voice. This is an opportunity to speak to what you couldn't in the past. Use the following prompts to get you started:
   - What hurts the most about the lack or loss?
   - What has this lack/loss cost you?
   - What do you wish someone had said or done?

3. **Offer care to the grieving part**
   Notice where you feel this grief in your body. What might bring you comfort now? Even small gestures, like a self-hug or making yourself a cup of tea, can help your system recognize that this pain is being acknowledged and witnessed with compassion.

EXERCISE 31

Operating from an Open Heart

WHAT YOU WILL NEED

A quiet space

Something to write with (optional)

A notebook or journal (optional)

TIME NEEDED

~20 minutes

The Change Triangle®, developed by Hilary Jacobs Hendel, is a powerful tool for understanding your emotions and moving toward your most authentic self. It helps you notice your defenses and work through inhibitory emotions to reconnect with your core emotions, process them, and move toward your authentic self, which she defines as the Openhearted State.

> **Tuning In**
>
> Check in with your window of tolerance, identify your grounding tools, and pause or seek support from a therapist if it begins to feel unmanageable.

Let's break down each element:

Core emotions: Naturally wired feelings, such as anger, fear, sadness, or joy. They appear automatically in response to your surroundings. When you recognize and experience them, they can pass through you, getting you to the Openhearted State.

Inhibitory emotions: A subset of feelings that block core emotions. They develop when core emotions feel too intense, or when they receive judgment from important people in your life like a parent, partner, or peers. They tend to show up as shame, guilt, or anxiety.

Defenses: Behaviors that keep you from feeling both inhibitory and core emotions. These include perfectionism, overworking, numbing, self-criticism, addictions, and people-pleasing. They may help you feel protected in the moment, but in reality, they keep you deeply disconnected.

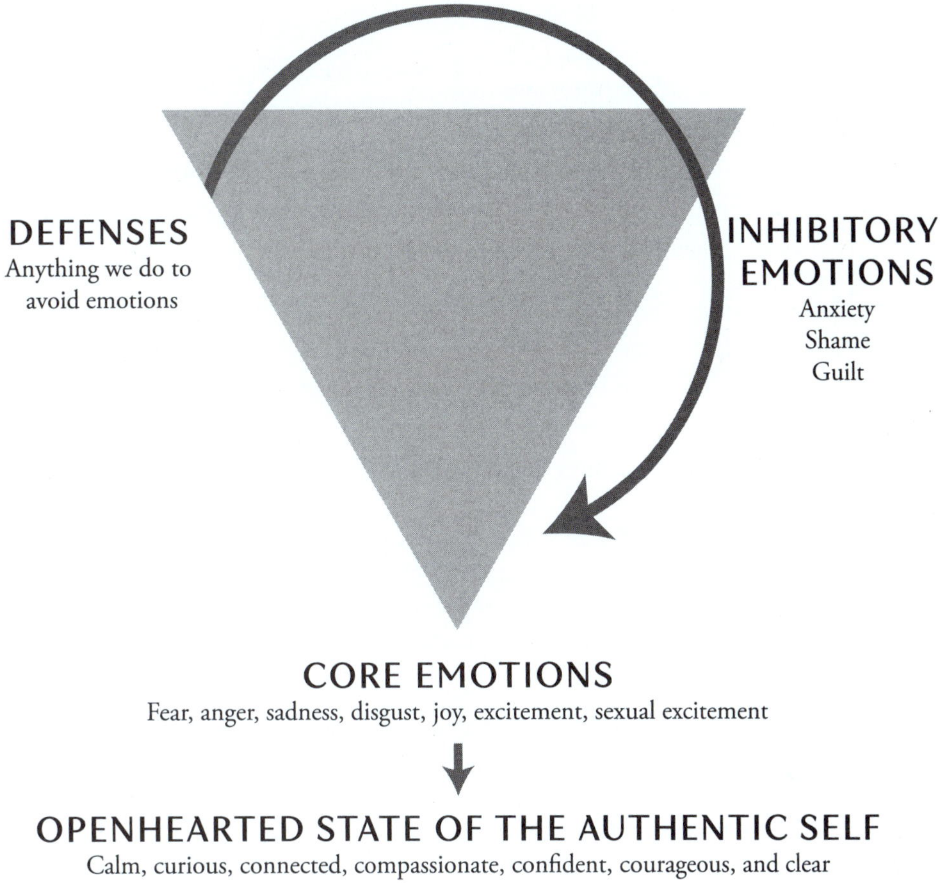

Repeat this exercise any time you notice the presence of a defense or inhibitory emotion, or when you want to practice riding the wave of a core emotion. After sitting with your core emotions, you may find yourself in your Openhearted State with more clarity.

(For more on the Change Triangle®, you can visit hilaryjacobshendel.com or read the book It's Not Always Depression *by Hilary Jacobs Hendel.)*

1. **Ground yourself**
   Allow yourself to pause, breathe, and ground yourself for a few seconds.

2. **Find where you are on the Change Triangle**
   Where are you currently? What resonates?

3. **Identify the underlying core emotions**

   When in a defensive or inhibitory emotion state, try to identify the underlying core emotions. You might drop into your body and notice any physical sensations representative of an emotional state. You might also ask yourself, "Is there anger here? Is there sadness here? Is there fear here?"

4. **! Stay with sensations of one core emotion**

   What are your core emotions trying to communicate to you? Remember, they are perfectly natural responses to your environment—a part of being human. When you validate and accept them, it's easier to sense them in the body, and stay with the sensations.

5. **Decide how to proceed**

   Do you want to listen to your core emotions, or move forward despite them? For example, if your partner goes on a trip with friends, you may feel anxious and have an underlying fear of abandonment. Your fear is telling you to text and call repeatedly. Your Openhearted State wants you to trust the security of your relationship and to tolerate the fear. Remind yourself that if the worst-case scenario were to happen, you would be able to survive it.

! EXERCISE 32

Making Sense of Experiences

WHAT YOU WILL NEED

Something to write with

A notebook or journal

TIME NEEDED

~30 minutes

Once you've given yourself space to feel and work through your emotions, your brain begins to shift out of "alarm mode" and back into a calmer, clearer state. This ability to think through and make sense of your experiences is vital because it transforms raw, overwhelming feelings into a coherent narrative your mind can integrate.

That integration is what allows you to loosen trauma's grip, reduce its emotional intensity, and begin building new meanings. Research suggests that simply writing about traumatic memories can improve mood, enhance outlook, strengthen immune functioning, and even lower blood pressure.

1. **Release through writing**
   Take some time to journal about the following:
   - Any facts and details of a traumatic event
   - Any thoughts, images, physical sensations, or emotions that you experienced during the event
   - Any thoughts, images, physical sensations, or emotions that you have about the event now
   - The impact you believe this has had on your life

2. **Suspend judgment; continue to write freely**
   As you do this exercise, try to suspend any judgment, self-expectation, or inner-critic talk. You'll know it's your inner critic if it sounds something like, "You should just get over it," or "You should have been stronger/better." Let this be a free flow of what your brain needs to express. Let it take you wherever it needs to take you.

PART III

Exercises for Expansion

Chapter 8

Practicing Self-Compassion

By giving ourselves unconditional kindness and comfort while embracing the human experience, difficult as it is, we avoid destructive patterns of fear, negativity, and isolation.

—KRISTIN NEFF

AS YOUR SENSE OF SAFETY and self-love grows, so too does your capacity to show up more fully in your relationships, take meaningful risks, and create a life that feels aligned with who you are. Building a foundation of self-trust and emotional resilience allows you to go after what you truly want.

The purpose of these exercises is to strengthen the belief "I deserve good things," and, eventually, "I can handle what life brings." They are an invitation to—without minimizing your pain—make peace with challenging aspects of your life experience and expand your capacity to love the most important person in your life: you.

! CLIENT STORY: PERMISSION TO TAKE UP SPACE

Ashanti grew up with a neglectful mother and an absent father, but much of her trauma stemmed from being hypersexualized beginning in middle school. She attended a combined middle and high school and went through puberty earlier than many of her peers, which led to unwanted attention from older students—attention that, at just 12 years old, she was not developmentally equipped to understand or manage.

When the attention turned into abuse, the school became involved. But, instead of supporting her, they blamed her. Repeated experiences of victim-blaming from teachers reinforced a core belief: "It's my fault." Over time, that belief expanded into deeper narratives like "I don't deserve good things" and "I'm a bad person."

Despite these early experiences, Ashanti always loved school and had big dreams. However, her shame and self-blame made it difficult for her to believe she could achieve what she truly wanted—healthy relationships, self-confidence, and a sense of self-worth that allowed her to pursue her passions. Through trauma work, she was able to process what happened, place responsibility where it belonged (on both the perpetrators and the systems that failed her), and rebuild a more compassionate relationship with herself. As her confidence and self-regulation grew, so did her willingness to take up space in the world. Ashanti recently landed her dream job. And for the first time, she truly believes she deserves it.

! EXERCISE 33

Finding Strength in Symptoms

WHAT YOU WILL NEED

Something to write with

A notebook or journal

TIME NEEDED

~25 minutes

Many of the things we criticize ourselves for, like shutting down, over-thinking, and people-pleasing, are survival strategies that helped us cope with overwhelming experiences. In trauma recovery, it's essential to recognize that what we call "symptoms" often began as strengths and intelligent adaptations to manage unbearable situations. This exercise helps shift the lens from shame to self-understanding.

> **Tuning In**
>
> This exercise asks you to reflect on coping patterns that may carry some shame or judgment. Before you begin, ask yourself if you can reflect without self-blame, and if you have access to self-compassion.

1. **Name up to three symptoms you've dealt with**
   These could be behaviors, thought patterns, or emotional responses linked to trauma. *Examples: people-pleasing, dissociation, anxiety or hypervigilance, over-controlling, numbing and avoidance strategies, and emotional outbursts*

2. **Reframe each one as a survival strategy**
   Ask yourself:
   - What was this part of me trying to do?
   - How did it protect me?
   - What skill or capacity is hidden in this pattern?

   Examples:

   People-pleasing → kept me safe in unsafe environments

   Dissociation → helped me escape emotional overwhelm

   Over-controlling → gave me a sense of predictability when everything felt chaotic

A NOTE ON REFRAMING

Some patterns may have caused harm to you or others. This exercise is not about labeling harmful behaviors as strengths, but rather about understanding how even the most distressing behaviors often started as attempts to meet the fundamental needs of safety, regulation, connection, and escape.

For example:

Self-harm → a way to feel something when numbness took over, or to release emotional intensity that felt unbearable

Substance use → a way to escape pain, regulate overwhelming emotions, or feel connected in moments of deep loneliness

Lashing out → a way to protect yourself from vulnerability, reclaim power, or signal distress when you didn't have other tools

There is an important difference between understanding and justifying. Compassionate reframing creates space to shift your relationship with these behaviors from one of shame or self-blame to one of choice and growth.

3. **Reflect**
    - Which of these patterns were trying to protect, soothe, or support you, even in messy or painful ways?
    - What strengths might have been buried inside them, like sensitivity, loyalty, resilience, creativity, or emotional depth?
    - Which of these strengths can you carry forward in healthier ways now?
    - How might your survival strategies be pointing you toward your deeper needs and values that are still seeking expression?

! EXERCISE 34

Writing a Self-Forgiveness Letter

WHAT YOU WILL NEED

Something to write with

A notebook or journal

TIME NEEDED

~20 minutes

Self-forgiveness is about approaching yourself with gentleness and compassion, rather than shame and punishment. This exercise is meant to help you practice internal repair to improve your relationship with yourself. Rewrite and/or reread this letter as many times as needed. The goal is to approach yourself with compassion and to permit yourself to stop punishing yourself for surviving.

> ### Tuning In
> This exercise may bring up feelings of guilt or shame. Check in with your window of tolerance, and make sure you have access to your grounding tools. Pause or skip this exercise if feeling overwhelmed or shut down.

1. **Attune to yourself**
   Settle into your space. If it feels comfortable, close your eyes or place a hand on your heart. Bring to mind a moment you're having trouble forgiving yourself for. It might be recent or from long ago. Just notice what arises.

2. **Write a letter to yourself**
   Write a short letter to the version of yourself that made that decision or acted that way, with the knowledge you now have about trauma's protective mechanisms. You may want to start with the following phrases:

   I know you were trying to ______________________________

   ____

   ____

   ____

I see how much pain you were in when ______________________________

____

____

You didn't have the tools you needed when ______________________

____

____

You deserved support, not shame, when _________________________

____

____

I forgive you for ____

____

____

You needed ____

____

____

____

3. **(Optional) The release ritual**
   Some people find it meaningful to symbolically release the letter by tearing or safely burning it as a way to let go of old blame, shame, or guilt that no longer needs to be carried. If this feels supportive, you can create a ritual around this. Others choose to keep the letter somewhere safe and visible as a symbol of their growth and healing process, and to keep practicing self-compassion.

! EXERCISE 35

Creating Your Resilience Timeline

WHAT YOU WILL NEED

Something to write with

A notebook or journal

TIME NEEDED

~40 minutes

Trauma often distorts our self-perception. You might remember the pain vividly but forget the strength it took to survive it. This practice helps you re-author your story by highlighting your capacity for resilience, courage, and growth. Even in the hardest chapters, you were moving forward. This timeline is intended to help you see that.

Tuning In

This exercise invites you to revisit difficult and defining moments from your past, which can stir up dysregulation. Before you continue, take a brief pause and check in with yourself. It's okay to skip this exercise and come back to it later.

1. **Draw your timeline**
   Sketch a horizontal line across a page. Write down six meaningful phases, such as childhood, high school, young adulthood, adulthood, after trauma, recovery, or today.

2. **Note what was hard and what helped you cope**
   Under each phase, write what was happening and what got you through. Reflect on your strengths, your choices, and your instincts.
   - What did you do to survive this phase?
   - What traits or values helped you get through?
   - What part of you was doing the heavy lifting?

3. **Identify patterns of strength**
   Look at the timeline as a whole and notice any repeating strengths that show up again and again. Are there moments when you made brave or quiet choices to protect yourself? What helped you keep going, even when things felt impossible?

4. **Reflect**
   What can you carry forward from this timeline as you step into your next chapter? What would you say now to the version of you who got through it?

EXERCISE 36

Building Joy as Resistance

WHAT YOU WILL NEED

Something to write with

A notebook or journal

TIME NEEDED

~20 minutes, with ongoing practice

In cPTSD recovery, joy becomes a form of quiet rebellion against the belief that safety is the only thing worth striving for. Joy points you toward what makes life worth living and strengthens your sense of purpose. Choosing joy is about expanding your story to also include pleasure. In this way, joy is both a tool for healing (see Exercise 9, p. 68) and a quiet act of resistance against anyone who tried to take it away from you.

1. **Name joyful moments**
   Think of at least five moments, big or small, when you felt genuine joy. These might include laughter with a friend, the feeling of sun on your face, or finishing a creative project. Write them down.

2. **Identify themes**
   Look at your list and notice any patterns. Do your joyful moments involve connection? Nature? Movement? Creativity?

3. **Plan your joyful practice**
   Choose one joyful activity that you can intentionally make space for in the next week, even for just 10 minutes. Schedule it like you would a nonnegotiable appointment.

EXERCISE 37

Tapping in Affirmations

WHAT YOU WILL NEED

A space with minimal interruptions

TIME NEEDED

~5–10 minutes

This practice uses Emotional Freedom Technique (EFT), which involves gently tapping specific acupressure points while repeating a phrase that acknowledges your struggle and introduces compassion.

Research shows EFT can reduce the brain's and body's stress responses, increasing a felt sense of safety. By pairing this physiological regulation with affirmations, you can begin to minimize old shame and increase your capacity for self-love. Return to this practice any time you need to soften self-judgment or offer yourself kindness and compassion.

1. **Attune to current experience**
   What emotions are you feeling toward yourself right now? Notice how strongly you feel the emotions before beginning.

2. **Choose an affirmation**
   Pick a short affirmation you'd like to gently tap in. It might feel true right now, or it might feel like something you hope to believe in the future. *Examples: "I'm allowed to take up space," "I am worthy of care."*

3. **Set up the statement**
   While tapping the side of your hand, repeat your version of: "Even though I feel [insert emotion] right now, [insert affirmation]."

   Example: "Even though I feel guilty right now, I deserve to set boundaries and protect myself."

   Repeat 2–3 times.

4. **Tap through the points**
   Continue tapping through each point 5–7 times while repeating your affirmation.

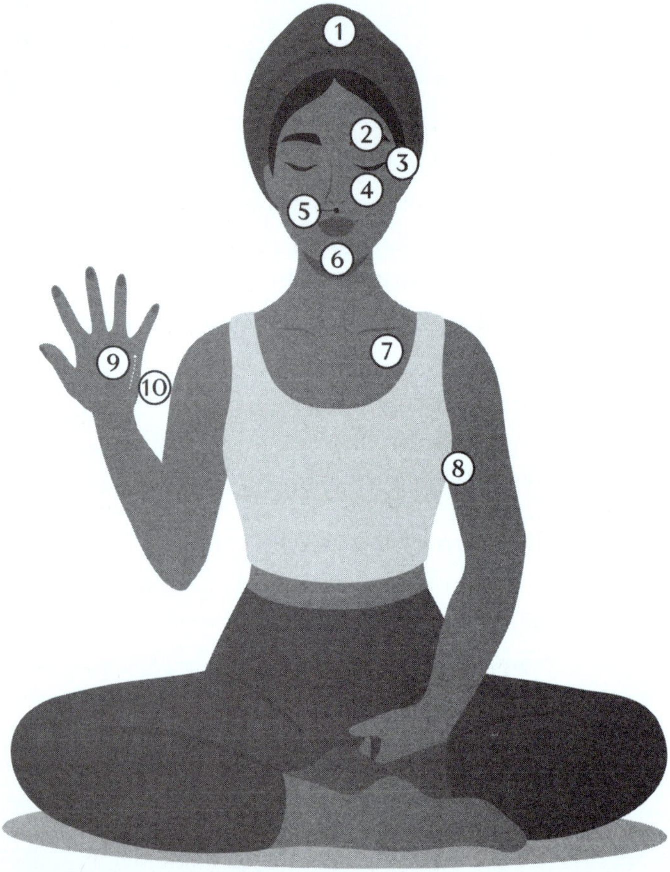

1.	Top of head	**6.**	Chin
2.	Eyebrow	**7.**	Collarbone
3.	Side of eye	**8.**	Under arm
4.	Under eye	**9.**	Gamut point*
5.	Under nose	**10.**	Side of hand

**The gamut point is the groove that runs down the back of your hand between your pinky and ring finger.*

EXERCISE 38

Crafting Your Self-Care Card

WHAT YOU WILL NEED

Something to write with

A notebook or journal (optional)

TIME NEEDED

~20 minutes, with ongoing implementation

Self-love and emotional regulation both require a foundation of self-connection and attunement. That means knowing what you need *and* how to provide that for yourself. This exercise helps you reconnect with your needs, define what care means for you, and build a personalized and compassionate plan that supports your emotional well-being.

1. **Identify your true needs**
   What does your nervous system need more of right now? Check in with your body, emotions, and environment. Answer these questions based on what feels authentic to you—not anyone else.

   My body is asking for: ______________________

   My mind is asking for: ______________________

   My heart is asking for: ______________________

   I feel most grounded when I: ______________________

   I feel most loved when I: ______________________

2. **Design your self-care card**
   Based on the answers above, develop your self-care card with the following three tiers:

   Daily Micro-Care (5–15 minutes): The things you can realistically do most days, even when dysregulated or short on time.

   Examples: drinking water, stretching, stepping outside for fresh air, speaking to yourself with kindness

Restorative Care (20–60 minutes): These are the activities that help you regulate, reset, or reconnect with yourself.

Examples: journaling, cooking a nourishing meal, connecting with a loved one, listening to a podcast, taking a walk

Deep Care (1 hour or more): This care helps instill the internal belief "I am allowed to take up space." These might involve more intention or vulnerability.

Examples: saying "no" to something that drains you, attending a therapy appointment, investing time in a dream you have, planning a solo date

3. **Create a plan**
   Begin by choosing one micro-care practice you can gently try to do each day. Even if a part of you feels like you don't deserve care yet, let the action come first. Over time, begin layering in restorative and deep care at a pace that feels supportive.

   You might set a gentle goal like: "I'll try to incorporate one deep-care activity every ______ week(s)" or "Once a week, I'll check in to see which level of care I need most."

Day	Daily Micro-Care	Restorative Care	Deep Care

EXERCISE 39

Learning to Master a Project

WHAT YOU WILL NEED

Something to write with

A notebook or journal

TIME NEEDED

Variable

This exercise invites you to gently go outside of your comfort zone by engaging in small, intentional activities that promote a sense of accomplishment, without overwhelming yourself. Over time, consistently showing up for yourself in this way can help shift your internal narrative.

1. **Identify a project**
   Pick something that feels meaningful and engaging—that you'd feel proud to make progress on over time. This could involve training for a 5K, cooking more meals at home, or learning a creative skill. Choose something that feels sustainable. The more emotionally connected you are to the project, the more likely you are to keep showing up for it on difficult days.

2. **Identify an appropriate challenge**
   Rate the task on a 1–5 challenge scale:

   1 = easy

   5 = very hard

   Ideally, you want to aim around 3, where you can gently push yourself out of your comfort zone while it still feels achievable. As your confidence builds, you'll notice that what once felt like a 5 feels more like a 3. Mastery is built by stacking the wins that reinforce your capability.

3. **Do the task**
   Show up for the task with compassion and curiosity, even when your motivation is low. Each time you complete something challenging, especially when you didn't feel like it, you strengthen the belief that you are capable and resilient.
   - Track how you feel before, during, and after.
   - Notice any shifts in mood, self-talk, or confidence.

4. **Record Your Progress**

Day	Mastery Activity	Difficulty Level	Outcome/Win

EXERCISE 40

Honoring Your Tree

WHAT YOU WILL NEED

Something to write with

TIME NEEDED

~20 minutes

Just like a tree, you are made up of many parts. You have roots that ground you, a trunk that holds you steady, branches that reach toward possibility, and leaves that display your flourishing.

This exercise invites you to reflect on your post-traumatic growth journey by using the tree on the next page and filling it with words that represent your healing and growth. You'll map out the strengths, healthy beliefs, and possibilities that are growing out of what you've lived through. Use it as a reminder of how far you've come and who you're becoming.

1. **Add words and symbols to your tree**
   Each part of the tree holds a different reflection:
   - ROOTS: These are your foundations of strength. Write words, names, or symbols that represent what grounds you. *Examples: my children, community, faith, patience, therapy, breathwork*
   - TRUNK: This represents your core identity. Write phrases that capture your core truths and strengths that help you stand tall. *Examples: I am resilient, I can trust myself, I am becoming whole*
   - BRANCHES: These represent the possibilities and pathways of post-traumatic growth. On each branch, write one possibility or area of growth that has come from your recovery. *Examples: healthy relationships, creativity, leadership, setting boundaries*
   - FRUIT/FLOWERS: These represent what you are offering the world. Write what you are able to give back on these. *Examples: empathy, advocacy, love, wisdom*

2. **Reflect on what you've drawn**
   When you look at your tree, what stands out to you about who you've become? What parts of your tree feel the strongest right now, and what parts could use more care and attention?

EXERCISE 41

Envisioning Your Future Self

WHAT YOU WILL NEED

Something to write with

A notebook or journal (optional)

TIME NEEDED

~25 minutes

When you've been in survival mode for a long time, it can seem nearly impossible to picture a future version of yourself—especially one that feels safe and fulfilled. But visualizing that future self and hearing from her can provide powerful insight and hope. This exercise is about connecting with the version of you that exists beyond the work you're doing now. By giving that version a voice, you might find it's more within reach than you previously thought.

1. **Picture your future self**

   This version of you has already done the work you're doing now. She still struggles sometimes (because that's human), but she's found her footing. Imagine where she is:
   - How does she spend her days?
   - Who does she surround herself with?
   - What does she feel proud of, or grateful for?

2. **Write a letter**

   She knows everything you've been through, and she's deeply proud of you. Some optional prompts to get you started:

   I know what you're carrying, and I want you to know . . .

   Here's what I want you to remember when things feel hard . . .

   Please keep going because . . .

   What helped me most along the way was . . .

3. **Read it back**

   See what words land. You might underline or highlight any parts that feel especially meaningful, or make changes. If this brought up emotion, that's okay and expected. You're not likely to believe every word your future self says. But something in you imagined her. Let her help you keep sight of what you're working toward.

Chapter 9

Building Sturdy Relationships

Being able to feel safe with other people is probably the single most important aspect of mental health; safe connections are fundamental to meaningful and satisfying lives.

—BESSEL VAN DER KOLK

RELATIONAL HEALING ADDRESSES THE HEART of most original wounds surrounding safety, trust, and vulnerability. It can also be one of the most triggering aspects of the healing process. Many times, the healing journey goes relatively smoothly until a new relationship enters the fold and reactivates old wounds. This is why relational work comes *after* developing self-awareness around what's happening inside your mind and body, and dedicating time to attuning to your own needs first.

The goal of this chapter is to help you reconnect with others in ways that feel safe and supportive. The practices here focus on identifying your needs (in relationship), rebuilding trust, and setting and maintaining healthy boundaries. You'll also explore how to cultivate a supportive social network, and how to repair when conflict arises.

Because your trauma happened in relationship, healing must also happen in relationship. This is what's known as a *corrective emotional experience*—moments of genuine safety and connection that signal to your nervous system that it's safe to be close to others again.

! CLIENT STORY: FINDING SAFETY IN RELATIONSHIPS

Elizabeth, age 34, was sexually assaulted by a teacher during her adolescence. In the aftermath, she developed a common trauma response known as *repetition compulsion*. That's the unconscious drive to reenact aspects of a traumatic experience to "master" it, regain a sense of control, or return to a familiar emotional state. This pattern led her to seek unsafe situations that reinforced her trauma and made it harder to build healthy relationships.

After completing the trauma processing phase of our work together, we moved on to helping Elizabeth learn how to safely and meaningfully connect with others. This involved recognizing safe versus unsafe people, developing the ability to feel secure in healthy relationships, strengthening her boundary-setting skills, and increasing assertiveness. While she learned these tools in therapy, it was her ability to apply them in real-life relationships that helped her start building more secure attachments.

In addition to strengthening her one-on-one relationships, we also worked on deepening her connection to a broader community. This was especially important given the lack of support she experienced during the time of her assaults. Developing a sense of belonging not only helped Elizabeth feel supported, but it also began to undo her core trauma belief: "No one is safe." The most meaningful shift in her healing came from cultivating a healthy, reliable support system that challenged and replaced her long-held wound.

EXERCISE 42

Clarifying Your Relationship Values

WHAT YOU WILL NEED
Something to write with

TIME NEEDED
~25 minutes

What kind of relationships do you want to build moving forward? This exercise invites you to identify your relationship values, to notice when old patterns may be pulling you toward what's familiar rather than what's truly aligned with the life you want to create, and to develop boundaries that protect you.

> **Remember**
> Your values are the compass for your relationships, and your boundaries help keep that compass pointed toward security.

> **Tuning In**
> This exercise prompts you to reflect on past relationships, which may stir up painful emotions. Check in with your capacity and window of tolerance (p. 51) before proceeding.

1. **! Identify what's familiar**
   List the types of relationships, behaviors, or patterns you've historically been drawn to, even if they didn't serve you.
   Examples: people who needed saving, made you prove your worth, were emotionally unavailable, were chaotic or intense

2. **Identify what's healthy (and maybe new)**
   List the relationship qualities that feel healthy to you, even if they're unfamiliar, boring, or uncomfortable.

   Examples: people who respect your boundaries, are emotionally consistent, apologize and repair, uplift you

   ____

   ____

   ____

3. **Define and advocate for your relationship values**
   Choose 3–5 values that feel most important in your relationships moving forward. These could include:

   - Mutual respect
   - Kindness
   - Accountability
   - Playfulness
   - Emotional honesty
   - Reciprocity
   - Reliability
   - Shared growth
   - Consent
   - Other ________

   ____

   ____

   For each value, explore the following:

My Value	What It Looks Like in a Relationship	What Undermines This Value	How I'll Know I'm at My Limit	How I'll Advocate for This Value
Example: Emotional honesty	*We both share openly and take accountability*	*Avoidance, dishonesty, gaslighting*	*I feel confused, shut down, or like I'm second-guessing myself*	*"I want to talk openly, and I need honesty to feel safe continuing this conversation."*

EXERCISE 43

Receiving Love

WHAT YOU WILL NEED

A quiet space

A blanket, candle, or object that helps you feel comforted

Something to write with

TIME NEEDED

~10 minutes

This gentle meditation is designed to help you practice receiving love—from safe people, your future self, or even imaginary figures. You don't need to believe every word right away. This is about making space for the possibility that love is meant for you, too. If this exercise feels uncomfortable, that's completely normal. With practice, your capacity to receive love can expand.

1. **Begin the meditation**
   You can read this to yourself slowly, record it and play it back, or have someone read it to you.
   - Close your eyes and take a few deep breaths to relax.
   - Inhale deeply through your nose and exhale slowly through your mouth. Allow your breath to become steady and natural.
   - Imagine someone, real or imagined, who loves you deeply and gently. Picture them offering you a warm, nonjudgmental presence.
   - Hear them say or say to yourself the following phrases:

     May you feel safe.

     May you be happy.

     May you live with ease.

     May you be filled with love and kindness.

- Let those words wash over you like a warm light. Allow yourself to stay open to the idea. If it feels okay, repeat these to yourself, modifying them to suit your needs and intentions:

  I am open to receiving love.

  I am worthy of care.

  I don't have to earn love.

  I only have to receive it.

2. **Reflect on your words**
   When you're ready, return to your space and take a moment to check in. How did it feel to hear those words?

Originally drawn from the Buddhist practice of Metta Bhavana ("loving-kindness meditation").

! EXERCISE 44

Unlearning the Good Girl

WHAT YOU WILL NEED

Something to write with

TIME NEEDED

~30 minutes

The urge to people-please, over-accommodate, and stay quiet to avoid conflict is part of living with cPTSD. The "good girl" helped you survive. But you are allowed to take up space, to have needs, and to stop managing everyone else's comfort. This exercise enables you to get to know your inner "good girl," and gently begin to create space for other parts of you to step forward—the ones that value honesty, assertiveness, boundaries, and self-expression, even if it feels unfamiliar or uncomfortable.

1. **Meet your inner "good girl"**
   List the qualities, roles, or rules your "good girl" had to follow over the years.

   To be good, I had to ______________________________

   ____

   ____

   I was praised for ______________________________

   ____

   ____

   I was afraid of being seen as ______________________________

   ____

   ____

   This part of me still shows up when ______________________________

   ____

   ____

2. **Understand how she was protective**
   Your "good girl" likely held deep wisdom about how to stay safe in unsafe relationships. This step is about honoring her by learning about her origins.

   This part believed that if I didn't fawn, then ______________________

   ____

   ____

   She helped me survive by ______________________________

   ____

   ____

   The cost of continuing to live this way is ______________________

   ____

   ____

3. **Imagine a more authentic self in a relationship**
   You don't have to abandon your "good girl," but you also don't need to let her run the show. Imagine what a healthy, mutual, honest connection could look like.

   If I didn't have to be "good," I would be ______________________

   ____

   ____

   I permit myself to ______________________________________

   ____

   In a healthy relationship, I want to show up as __________________

   ____

EXERCISE 45

Identifying Your Attachment Style

WHAT YOU WILL NEED
Something to write with

TIME NEEDED
~30 minutes, with ongoing practice

You may find yourself craving closeness but fearing it, pushing people away without meaning to, or feeling like your relationships are volatile. This exercise helps you explore your attachment style so you can build internal coherence and learn to trust that connection doesn't have to be chaotic. Knowing which one you align with can help you put words to confusing emotional reactions, offer clarity about your relationships, and open up a clear path toward building secure relationships.

1. **Check off your patterns**
   On the following page are four quadrants, each one an everyday attachment style. Read through each one and check off the items that resonate. You might relate to more than one quadrant—that's normal.

2. **Reflect**

   Which quadrant had the most checkmarks?

   ____

   How do these patterns show up in your romantic relationships, friendships, or professional dynamics?

   ____

   Where might you want to grow more secure in your connections?

   ____

3. **Move toward secure attachment**
   The good news is that attachment styles can shift with awareness and practice. The focus areas on the next page tend to help people move toward more secure attachment, depending on their original attachment style.

Secure

- ☐ I feel comfortable getting close to others.
- ☐ I trust people to care about me even when we're apart.
- ☐ I'm able to express my needs and listen to others' needs.
- ☐ I can handle conflict without feeling overwhelmed or abandoned.
- ☐ I believe I'm worthy of love and connection.
- ☐ I can ask for help when I need it.
- ☐ I give and receive support without guilt or fear.

Anxious

- ☐ I often worry that people will leave me or stop caring.
- ☐ I feel "too much" in relationships.
- ☐ I tend to overanalyze texts, tone, or silence.
- ☐ I need frequent reassurance to feel secure.
- ☐ I sometimes lose myself when trying to please or keep people close.

Avoidant

- ☐ I feel safest when I don't rely on others.
- ☐ Emotional closeness often makes me feel overwhelmed.
- ☐ I need a lot of space in relationships.
- ☐ I tend to downplay my needs or emotions.
- ☐ I withdraw when things get too intense.
- ☐ I often feel burdened when people depend on me.
- ☐ I value independence over vulnerability.

Disorganized

- ☐ I want connection but also fear it.
- ☐ I sometimes push people away even when I want closeness.
- ☐ My responses to relationships feel unpredictable, even to me.
- ☐ I grew up with inconsistent or unsafe caregivers.
- ☐ I'm afraid of being hurt or controlled in relationships.
- ☐ I alternate between needing people and needing to escape them.
- ☐ Intimacy feels dangerous and confusing.

If you lean **anxious:** Your work is in learning to self-soothe and trust your worth, even when others feel distant or unclear.

Practice: Pausing before reaching out for reassurance.

Goal: Anchor into your sense of security within, instead of seeking it only externally.

If you lean **avoidant:** Your task is to risk healthy vulnerability by letting others in, even when it feels safer to go at it alone.

Practice: Naming a feeling or asking for help, even in small ways.

Goal: Allow closeness without feeling engulfed.

If you lean **disorganized:** Your healing involves building emotion regulation and learning that relationships can be safe and stable.

Practice: Tracking your reactions to build insight into your triggers, and grounding yourself during moments of overwhelm.

Goal: Self-regulate when navigating a trigger and strengthen sense of safety in relationships.

EXERCISE 46

Checking the Facts

WHAT YOU WILL NEED

Something to write with

TIME NEEDED

~20–30 minutes

Complex trauma often rewires the nervous system to be hypervigilant. This is your brain trying to protect you from past trauma, even if the threat isn't there anymore. Checking the facts doesn't mean invalidating your feelings—your emotional reactions always make sense in the context of your story. But, when you're emotionally activated, it can help to ask, "Is this emotion fully about what's happening now, or is it touching on something older?" This enables you to slow down, practice emotional control, and respond with intention.

1. **Identify the emotion you want to change**
   What is the emotion you are currently experiencing that you would like to reduce at this time?

   ____

   ____

   ____

   ____

2. **What just happened?**
   Briefly describe the situation that triggered the emotion. Jot down what you observed.

   ____

   ____

   ____

   ____

   Example: My friend canceled our plans last minute. She texted me an hour before we were supposed to meet, saying she wasn't feeling well.

3. **What story are you telling yourself?**

What are your interpretations, thoughts, and assumptions about the event?

____

____

____

What are all the other sides and points of view?

____

____

____

Do your assumptions and interpretations fit the facts? _______________

____

____

Challenge any judgments, absolutes, or black-and-white thinking.

____

____

____

Example: I noticed I was thinking, "She doesn't value our friendship," but that's an assumption. It's possible she really is sick or had something unexpected come up.

4. **Are you assuming a threat or a catastrophe?**

What threat or catastrophe are you assuming? _______________

____

____

____

Assess the probability that the threat will really occur. ______

______

______

______

Imagine coping really well with a disaster. ______

______

______

______

Think of as many other possible outcomes as you can. ______

______

______

______

Example: I'm worried this means she's pulling away from me, and we'll stop being friends. However, she's canceled before when she was sick, and we still see each other regularly. If our friendship did fade, I could focus on my other relationships and meet new people. Realistically, she probably genuinely is sick and might need a quiet night at home. We can reschedule for later next week.

5. **Does your emotion (and its intensity) fit the facts?**
   - If **yes**, that means your emotions fit the moment. Move toward problem-solving, setting boundaries, or practicing radical acceptance for anything outside of your control.
   - If **no**, that doesn't mean your feelings aren't valid—it just means your mind and body are responding to past wounds.

6. **Pause and ground yourself**
   Before making any decisions or reacting, ask yourself, "What would help me feel more at ease right now?" Take a moment to self-soothe, using any tools that feel natural to you, or pulling from your grounding toolkit (Exercise 3, p. 59).

EXERCISE 47

Asking for What You Need

WHAT YOU WILL NEED

Something to write with

A notebook or journal

TIME NEEDED

~15–20 minutes to draft your script, with ongoing implementation

It can feel intimidating to ask for what you need after trauma, especially if your boundaries were repeatedly crossed. This exercise, as well as the two that follow, will provide DBT-inspired tools to advocate for yourself while maintaining personal relationships. The DEAR MAN approach helps you communicate clearly and respectfully while increasing the chance that your needs will be heard.

1. **Identify the situation.**
   Choose a current example—perhaps asking your partner for more help at home or requesting a deadline extension at work.

2. **Use the DEAR MAN structure.**

   D—Describe the facts without judgment.

   E—Express how you feel and what you need.

   A—Assert your request clearly.

   R—Reinforce how this benefits both of you.

   M—Mindful: stay focused on your goal.

   A—Appear confident: steady tone, open posture.

   N—Negotiate if compromise is needed.

3. **Write out your script/plan**

   Example:

   Script Part 1: "When the dishes pile up (Describe), I feel overwhelmed and stressed (Express). I need help keeping the kitchen clean (Assert). It'll make our evenings calmer for both of us (Reinforce)."

   Plan: I'll keep my voice calm if the conversation gets tense, and focus solely on discussing the dishes right now (Mindful). I'll speak clearly and kindly (Appear confident).

   Script Part 2: "If weekdays are tough, maybe you can handle weekends (Negotiate)."

4. **Practice your script**

   Review your script and plan. Practice aloud, adjusting until it feels natural.

EXERCISE 48

Strengthening Relationships

WHAT YOU WILL NEED

Something to write with

A notebook or journal

TIME NEEDED

~15–20 minutes to draft your script, with ongoing implementation

When connection matters more than being "right," GIVE helps you keep relationships strong. It's especially useful when you want to stay kind and present with people you love and care about. Use GIVE when preserving closeness and trust is your top goal.

1. **Identify the relationship and situation**
   Think of a relationship where the person is important to you but communication sometimes feels tense or distant.

2. **Apply the GIVE skill**

   G—Gentle: Speak with kindness, no attacks or threats.

   I—Interested: Listen and show genuine curiosity.

   V—Validate: Acknowledge the other person's feelings.

   E—Easy manner: Stay relaxed, use warmth or light humor.

3. **Write your script**
   Example: "I know this topic is tough (Gentle). Can you tell me what's been hardest for you (Interested)? I understand why you'd feel frustrated—it makes sense (Validate). Let's take a breath before we keep talking (Easy manner)."

4. **Practice your script**
   Practice aloud, adjusting until it feels natural.

EXERCISE 49

Protecting Your Self-Respect

WHAT YOU WILL NEED

Something to write with

A notebook or journal

TIME NEEDED

~15–20 minutes to draft your script, with ongoing implementation

Trauma can make self-respect feel negotiable. FAST helps you honor your values while communicating firmly and fairly. Use FAST when you risk losing self-respect or people-pleasing at your own expense.

1. **Identify the issue**
   Pick a situation where you often apologize or abandon your needs to avoid conflict.

2. **Apply the FAST skill**

   F—Fair: Be fair to yourself and the other person.

   A—(No) Apologies: Only apologize when truly warranted.

   S—Stick to your values: Hold your boundaries.

   T—Truthful: Be honest, without exaggeration or excuse.

3. **Write your script**
   Example: "I understand you're disappointed (Fair). It's important to me to take time for myself—rest is part of how I stay healthy (No apologies; Stick to values). I promised myself to prioritize balance this year (Truthful)."

4. **Practice your script**
   Practice aloud, adjusting until it feels natural.

EXERCISE 50

Choosing Which Skill to Use

WHAT YOU WILL NEED

Your completed scripts or journal notes

TIME NEEDED

~10 minutes of reflection

It's common to feel unsure of how to navigate conflict and communication after enduring ongoing trauma. Now that you've practiced DEAR MAN, GIVE, and FAST, this exercise helps you determine which one fits best in the moment. You can use one at a time, or sometimes you'll blend two or all three. Practice helps you flex between them based on what feels most aligned.

1. **Revisit a recent interaction**
   Think of a conversation that didn't go the way you hoped.
2. **Ask yourself what mattered most**

If you cared most about . . .	Use . . .
Being heard, getting needs met	DEAR MAN
Preserving the relationship	GIVE
Staying true to yourself	FAST

3. **Reflect**
   Which skill best fits that situation? Could combining two help (e.g., DEAR MAN + GIVE when you want to ask for something while maintaining warmth)?
   Example: "When I asked for help moving, I could have used DEAR MAN to make the request and GIVE to stay warm. It would have felt more balanced and less tense."
4. **Apply and review**
   Use your chosen skill in a low-stakes conversation this week. Afterward, note what felt natural and what felt challenging.

EXERCISE 51

Practicing Rupture and Repair

WHAT YOU WILL NEED

Something to write with

A notebook or journal

TIME NEEDED

~30 minutes, with ongoing practice

For many trauma survivors, conflict still feels like danger. However, in safe and secure relationships, conflict is an opportunity for repair. When done thoughtfully, repair can build trust and deepen intimacy. It teaches you that you can be on different wavelengths and still love one another. This exercise helps you explore your relationship to conflict, understand what repair looks like for you, and practice scripts to either offer or ask for repair.

1. **Identify your rupture patterns**

   Think about how you usually respond.

   When something feels "off" in a relationship, I tend to . . .

   That's because . . .

   A part of me is afraid that if I show I'm hurt . . .

2. **Define what repair feels like to you**

   What helps rebuild trust?

   What helps me feel soothed after I've been hurt?

   What gestures or actions feel genuine?

   What feels dismissive or unsafe, even when someone says "sorry"?

3. **Write your scripts**

RECEIVING REPAIR:

What would you want someone to say to you after they've hurt you?

"When you ________, I felt ________. I really needed ________.

I wish I could hear ________."

Example: "When you didn't respond to my message, I felt ignored and anxious. I really needed some acknowledgment. I wish I could hear 'I'm sorry I didn't respond—I didn't mean to leave you hanging.'"

OFFERING REPAIR:

Now imagine you've made a mistake. You want to take responsibility without over-apologizing or spiraling into shame. Try this structure: acknowledge, validate, take responsibility, and offer repair.

"I can see how ______ really hurt you, and I'm sorry. I was feeling ______, but that doesn't excuse it. I want to learn from this and do better."

Example: "I can see how ignoring your calls really hurt you, and I'm sorry. I was feeling overwhelmed, but that doesn't excuse it. I want to learn from this and do better."

4. **Identify what gets in the way**

Explore what's underneath:

A part of me believes that if I speak up about my hurt, then . . .

A part of me believes that if I admit I was wrong, then . . .

But I'm learning that healthy relationships can handle . . .

EXERCISE 52

Finding Community

WHAT YOU WILL NEED

Something to write with

TIME NEEDED

~20 minutes, with ongoing implementation

You may have been taught to prioritize others' needs over your own, maintain peace at all costs, or stay silent when something felt wrong. Over time, these experiences can feel profoundly isolating. Research shows that belonging reduces the physical and emotional burdens of trauma. Strong social connections are associated with better emotion regulation, fewer symptoms, and even improved immune function. Community support helps buffer stress and reminds you that you have always mattered.

1. **Redefine what "community" means to you**
   Check off what resonates, or add your own:
   - ☐ Close friendships
   - ☐ Support groups or therapy groups
   - ☐ Identity-based spaces (LGBTQ+, BIPOC, spiritual)
   - ☐ Shared interests (book club, yoga, activism)
   - ☐ Online spaces
   - ☐ Creative or cultural spaces
   - ☐ Other: ____________________

2. **Name where you already feel a spark**
   Who or what already feels even a little safe or nourishing? List 3–5 people, spaces, or groups.

   ____

   ____

   ____

   ____

3. **Identify what you're craving more of**
   What kind of connection are you most longing for?
   - ☐ Consistency
   - ☐ Emotional safety
   - ☐ Joy or play
   - ☐ Shared purpose
   - ☐ Belonging
   - ☐ Other: ______________________________

4. **Take one gentle step forward**
   List one small action you could take toward more connection: __________

   ____

Community doesn't always appear in the ways we expect. Sometimes it begins as a shared interest or a familiar face in a new space. Take small steps to build safe-enough connections.

If you're ready to explore, here are a few starting points:

MEETUP.COM—Find in-person or virtual events based on your interests (support groups, walking meetups, creative gatherings, etc.)

EVENTBRITE.COM—Search free and low-cost community events in your area

REDDIT–R/CPTSD—Peer support, stories, and shared tools for those navigating complex trauma

PSYCHOLOGYTODAY.COM/US/GROUPS—Local and online therapy and support groups

LOCAL ORGANIZATIONS—Check your area for women's centers, LGBTQ+ and BIPOC spaces, trauma-informed yoga or meditation studios, or mutual aid groups

Chapter 10

Thriving in Wholeness

Healing is the return of the memory of wholeness.

—DEEPAK CHOPRA

THE CPTSD YOU EXPERIENCE ISN'T only about what happened in the past; it's about how those experiences still shape your present. Healing means reclaiming the parts of yourself you had to set aside and learning to live from a place of wholeness rather than fragmentation. This chapter focuses on thriving in wholeness—living as your most authentic, embodied self. This means nurturing self-love, connection, and joy—feeling grounded enough to move toward what you hope for with curiosity and embracing life without waiting for the other shoe to drop.

Here, you'll find practices that help you reconnect with vitality and direction, rediscover play and pleasure, and cultivate a life that feels safe, meaningful, and fully your own. You deserve more than survival—you deserve a life that feels whole and alive.

! CLIENT STORY: LIVING BEYOND OTHERS' EXPECTATIONS

Carolyn was in her thirties when she sought therapy to address repeated sexual trauma. When she first entered treatment, we focused on helping her gently regulate her nervous system and reduce harmful coping strategies. The goal was for her to begin processing the events that contributed to her profound sense of fragmentation.

As Carolyn gradually confronted her trauma, her protective parts no longer needed to work so hard. Her future seemed possible. She began reconnecting with the aspects of herself she had long pushed away. By clarifying her own values and stepping outside her comfort zone, Carolyn was working to create a life that felt true to her, rather than one shaped by others' expectations.

This process started gaining momentum. The more she embraced her strengths, the more confident and grounded she felt. With each step, Carolyn's confidence grew, enabling her to keep pursuing a life that reflected her true self. This involved leaving a toxic work environment, ending a romantic relationship where she was mistreated, and launching the creative small business she had always dreamed of. This phase of her healing was transformative, helping her begin to regain the self-worth and self-esteem she had lost after her trauma.

EXERCISE 53

Seeing the Mosaic of Me

WHAT YOU WILL NEED

Something to write with

A notebook or journal

Colored pencils or collage materials, if you want to make it visual

TIME NEEDED

~30–45 minutes

After trauma, it's common to feel fragmented—like different parts of you were created to cope, protect, hide, or survive. This exercise helps you reconnect with all those parts as a way of compassionately recognizing how they shaped you. By bringing these parts together, you begin to see your identity as complex and whole, like a mosaic. Over time, integrating these parts helps you reclaim a more stable sense of self.

> **Tuning In**
>
> This exercise asks that you connect with parts of yourself that you may hold discomfort or judgment toward. Pause here and take a few slow breaths. Give yourself permission to pause or skip this exercise if needed.

1. **Name your parts**
   - Think of the different parts of you that have emerged in response to your traumatic experiences and survival needs. *Examples: the perfectionist, the quiet one, the fixer, the dreamer, the angry one, the child, the skeptic, the creative, the teenager, the tactful one*
   - Give your parts names, roles, symbols, and images. Go with what feels intuitively true.
   - What are 3–6 parts of you that you'd like to include in your mosaic?

2. **Listen to their stories**

   For each part, write a sentence or two about what this part has done for you, what it was afraid of, and what it was trying to protect.

3. **Add the healing parts**

   Now, think of the parts of you that have started to emerge through healing. These might feel newer or less familiar, like confidence, compassion, boundaries, joy, or trust. What parts of you are stepping forward now?

4. **Build your mosaic**
   Now imagine all these parts fitting together as a complete picture of what makes you, you. You can draw them in a circle, grid, abstract pattern—whatever feels right. If you'd rather keep it written, simply describe how they relate.

5. **Reflect**
   What do you notice about yourself when you view all your parts as valid and valuable?

   What would it look like to lead your life from the "you" that holds all of these parts with compassion?

EXERCISE 54

Integrating Before- and After-Trauma Values

WHAT YOU WILL NEED

Something to write with

TIME NEEDED

~25 minutes

Values are like a compass. You may not always walk in a straight line, but your values can guide you back to what matters most. This exercise helps you reflect on the ways your core values may have shifted or deepened after trauma. It draws from post-traumatic growth research, which shows that people often find new purpose, authenticity, or appreciation for life after surviving hardship.

1. **! Gently look back**

   Consider the following questions:

   - What did I need or long for as a child? ____________________

     ____

   - What values or guiding principles felt most important to me then?

     ____

     ____

   - What qualities helped me get through hard times, even if I didn't name them as values back then?

     ____

     ____

   - What parts of me tried to hold on to hope, connection, fairness, or care, even in unsafe environments?

     ____

     ____

List 3–5 values, needs, or guiding instincts identified from the past:

2. **Consider who you are now**
   Now, take stock of your current values. Ask yourself:

   What do I care about more deeply now?

   What do I want to honor, protect, or move toward in this next chapter of life?

   Have any of my values shifted, deepened, or clarified since surviving trauma?

   List 3–5 values or guiding principles you hold now:

3. **Reflect**
   What changed between these two lists?

   Are there any values you've reclaimed or rediscovered?

   How can you live more in alignment with what matters most to you now?

! EXERCISE 55

Reclaiming Your Life Story

WHAT YOU WILL NEED

Something to write with

A notebook or journal

TIME NEEDED

~25 minutes

The story of who you've become because of how you showed up in your healing journey is important. This exercise is about reclaiming authorship over your life story and integrating it with the strength, values, and identity you've built throughout your recovery. This narrative therapy exercise asks you to reflect upon and write down your growth journey through the lens of your *personal integration statement.*

> ### Tuning In
> Reflecting on your trauma story and who you are now can bring up mixed emotions, including grief, pride, and sadness. Tune in with yourself before you begin. Do you need more regulation before proceeding with this exercise?

Instructions

Write your personal integration statement. This is not a summary of your trauma. This is a reflection of your growth, your identity, and the truth behind your experience. It's your opportunity to decide how to name what you've lived through, what it taught you, and who you choose to become from this point on.

Here's an example that may help demonstrate the difference between a trauma summary versus a growth reflection:

Trauma summary: "I was abandoned and betrayed, and it left me feeling unworthy."

Growth reflection: "I've learned that even when I've been abandoned, I can cultivate belonging within myself and in communities of my choosing."

Here are some prompts to get you started:

- What do I now know to be true?
- What parts of myself have I reclaimed?
- What will no longer define me?

EXERCISE 56

Drawing Your Wholeness Map

WHAT YOU WILL NEED

Pencil or colored pencils

TIME NEEDED

~30 minutes

I developed the Wholeness Map to help clients step back and look at the bigger picture of their life. I've found that from this vantage point, it's easier to see which areas feel solid and which might need more attention.

By exploring the different domains on the next page, you can clarify what's most important to you. This exercise is meant to offer a sense of direction by helping you choose where to invest your time and energy for the greatest sense of fulfillment. Its intent is to allow you to shape the life you want by making values-based choices that honor the whole of who you are today.

1. **Reflect on each domain**
   For each wedge, consider your responses to these prompts:
   - What does thriving in this area look like for me?
   - What type of person do I want to be?
   - How do I ideally want to behave?
2. **Color or shade your wedges**
   Use color or shading to indicate how aligned you feel with each area. The more filled in it is, the more aligned you feel with the area.
3. **Identify your top focus areas**
   Circle one or two wedges where you'd like to focus more attention over the next few months. Choose what feels meaningful and important, not just what feels urgent. Your values are the directions you keep moving toward, even when life takes you on detours. If you ever feel lost, you can return to this map to remind you what living in alignment looks like.

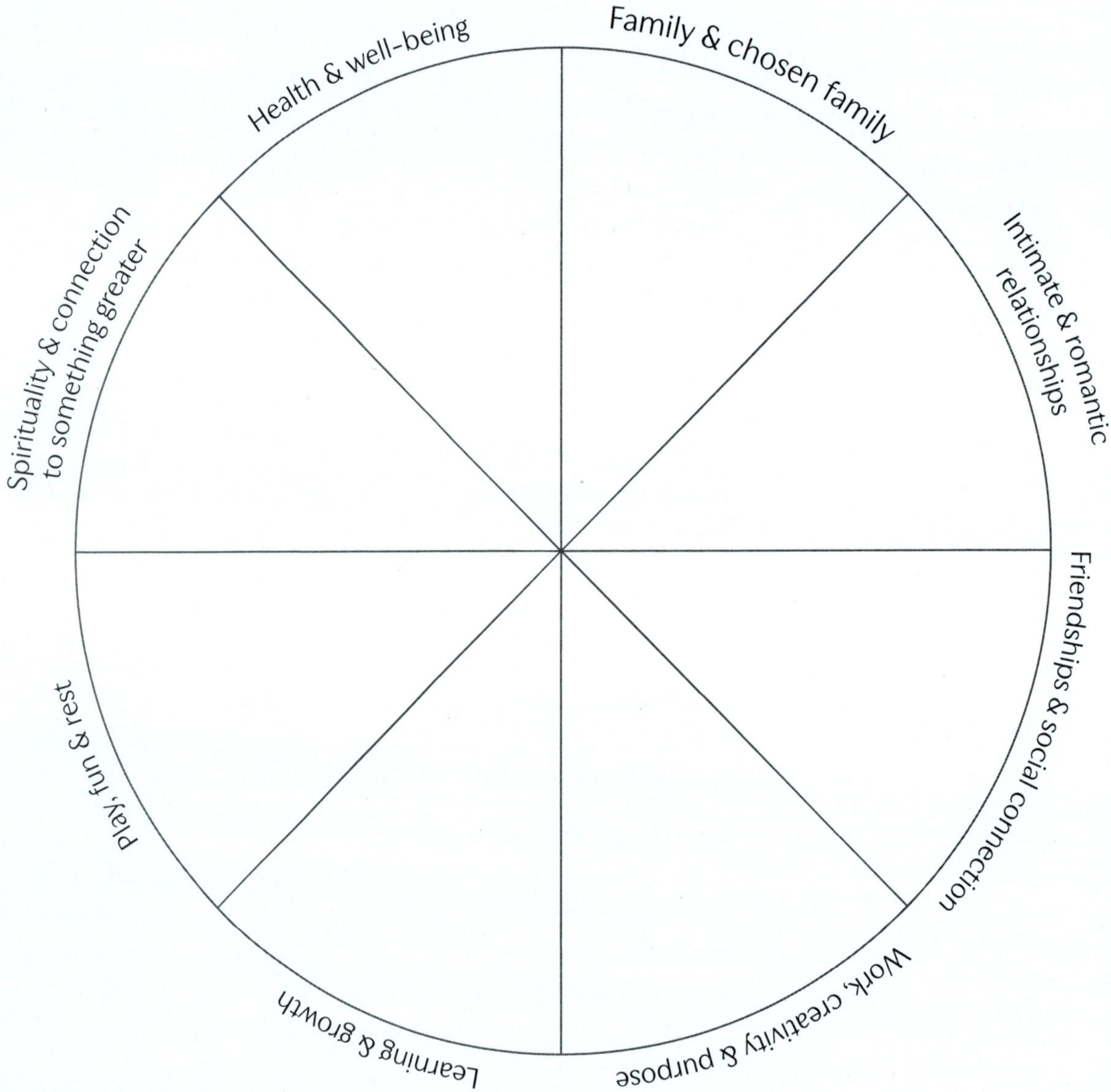
Health & well-being
Family & chosen family
Intimate & romantic relationships
Friendships & social connection
Work, creativity & purpose
Learning & growth
Play, fun & rest
Spirituality & connection to something greater

EXERCISE 57

Nurturing Life as a Garden

WHAT YOU WILL NEED

Something to write with

TIME NEEDED

~20–40 minutes, with ongoing practice

Planting a garden takes patience. You won't see results overnight, but consistent care eventually pays off in ways that feel lasting and deeply satisfying. Building a life that feels meaningful and worth living after trauma also takes patience.

This exercise draws your attention to the activities, habits, and commitments that you value but may not give you an instant sense of gratification. Over time, commitment to them can nurture a richer, more stable foundation for well-being.

1. **Identify your garden beds**
   Choose 4–6 areas of your life you want to nurture long term.
   Examples: relationships, health, personal growth, creativity, contribution, leisure

2. **Plant your seeds**

   For each area, list one activity, goal, or habit that would help it grow. Keep them realistic and specific to your current circumstances.

Area	Activity, Goal, or Habit for Growth

3. **Anticipate weeds**

Identify one or two challenges that might get in the way of each goal and write down a strategy for navigating them.

Area	Challenges	How You'll Navigate

4. **Nurture consistently**

Decide on one small action you can take this week to start moving toward one of these goals. Put it in your calendar to increase the likelihood that you'll follow through.

____

____

Adapted from Linehan, 2014.

EXERCISE 58

Clarifying Your Offering

WHAT YOU WILL NEED

A quiet, comfortable space

Something to write with

A notebook or journal

A candle, a meaningful object, or access to nature (optional)

TIME NEEDED

~30 minutes

When the daily work of coping no longer consumes all your energy, you may find yourself asking, "What now?" This exercise offers a secular, intentional ritual for transforming what you've learned into a conscious offering you place into the world. It symbolizes the way your personal growth can extend outward as you stay rooted in the person you've become through your healing journey.

1. **Set the space**
   Create a small ritual to mark the start. Light a candle, sit by a window, or place a hand on your heart.

2. **Reflect and write**
   - What has trauma taught me about what matters most?
   - What do I want to stand for in the world—whether loud or quiet, public or private?
   - What kind of presence do I want to be for others? Not as a fixer, but as someone who's grown something meaningful from pain?
   - What's one small way I can offer that forward?
   - Complete the sentence: Now that I've survived, I offer ________ to the world.

3. **The offering ritual**
   Choose how you'll "send forward" your offering: write it on paper and keep it somewhere meaningful, plant something symbolic, create art that expresses it, burn it, etc.

4. **Schedule your renewal**
   Schedule a date in your calendar (1–3 months from now) to revisit your offering. Ask, "Does this still reflect what I want to bring into the world? How has it shifted?" Allow yourself to adjust as needed, allowing this to be an evolving part of you.

EXERCISE 59

Making a Thriving Vision Board

WHAT YOU WILL NEED

Something to write with

(Physical option) Poster boards or a large sheet of paper, magazines or printed images, scissors, glue stick, pens/markers

(Digital option) Pinterest, Canva, or any digital collage app, with access to images

TIME NEEDED

~30–60 minutes

Vision boards help shift attention from past pain toward future possibilities, reinforcing a sense of hope. In fact, research on visualization suggests that visually representing goals can increase motivation and self-efficacy, especially when paired with planning and action. This exercise focuses on helping you clarify what you want and reconnecting with the possibility that it's available to you.

> **Tuning In**
> Imagining the future can stir feelings of grief. Check in with yourself, your window of tolerance, and any grounding needs before proceeding.

1. **Clarify your themes**
   Think about the core areas of life that matter most to you right now (e.g., relationships, health, creativity, home, purpose, leisure, personal growth). Write down 4–6 themes you'd like represented on your board.

   ____

   ____

   ____

   ____

   ____

2. **Gather your images**
   Flip through magazines or images that reflect your themes. Look for visuals that spark a sense of possibility and excitement. If you'd like, you can also create separate folders or boards for each theme.

3. **Create your board**
   Arrange your images on your board or digital canvas. Let it be intuitive. You might group themes together or scatter them around. Include words or short affirmations if they resonate.

4. **Add future planning**
   For each theme or image that's important to you, write down:

   Why this matters to you at this time

   One action step you can take in the next month to move closer to it

   Any possible obstacles that could make it harder, and plans to navigate it

5. **Place it where you'll see it**
   Put your vision board somewhere visible like a wall, or your phone or laptop background, so it can serve as a reminder of the life you're intentionally building. By pairing imagery with action planning, you're turning your vision board into a living tool for change. Every time you see it, let it remind you that you have a say in the life you're creating.

EXERCISE 60

Actualizing a Thriving Plan

WHAT YOU WILL NEED

Something to write with

TIME NEEDED

~45 minutes

Narrative therapy emphasizes that how you tell your story shapes how you live it. When you create an integration statement, you're consciously stepping into authorship of your life by acknowledging that trauma is part of your story, but it's not your entire story.

The integration statement you develop will also include concrete steps for building a life aligned with your values. This is called your Thriving Plan. Your statement isn't just about naming your post-trauma identity; it's also about turning that identity into action. By adding small, sustainable steps, you'll carry your growth off the page and into your daily life.

1. **Pull the story pieces together**
   Use the prompts below to gather the pieces of your story:

   Three strengths that helped me through recovery are

   ____

   ____

   ____

   ____

   ____

   The values that matter most to me now are

   ____

   ____

   ____

   ____

   ____

The lessons I've learned about myself are

One way I want to be in the world is

2. **Craft your integration statement**
   Using your responses from Step 1, create an expression of your post-trauma self. Tell your story in any way that feels authentic to you, reflecting both where you've been and where you're going.

   This can be as long or short as it needs to be. You might:

   - Write a letter to yourself about the life you're building.
   - Create a personal manifesto of values, strengths, and intentions.
   - Write a poem that captures your journey and your future.

3. **Create your Thriving Plan**

   List 3–5 small, tangible actions that align with your integration statement. Consider different life domains:

   - **Relationships:** How will I nurture supportive connections?
   - **Self-care:** How will I care for my mind, body, and emotions?
   - **Work and passions:** How will I bring my values into my professional or creative life?
   - **Play and joy:** How will I keep joy part of my routine?

Examples:

- *Schedule one monthly outing that brings me joy.*
- *Speak my needs clearly in important relationships.*
- *Keep one grounding tool in my bag at all times.*

Conclusion

Let's take a moment to recognize where you are, and how much you've done to take hold of your life. This book has asked you to face some of the most complex parts of your past, explore patterns that may have felt safer to avoid, and practice new ways of moving through the world. That requires courage and a willingness to sit with discomfort.

My clients often share that their most empowering healing happens in small, everyday experiences. These were the moments when they realized they could get through something hard without losing themselves in it. Their transformation was not the absence of struggle. It was the ability to build a life that allowed them to meet challenges while holding a clear, compassionate, and strong sense of self.

Healing from complex trauma is not a straight path. You may still have days when old wounds feel raw, when your nervous system is dysregulated, or when relationships challenge you in painful ways. The difference is that you've taken time to develop tools, insight, and a stronger foundation for responding to those moments—*in* those moments. The practices in this book are resources you can return to, deepen, or adapt over time. Think of them as roots that are strong and steady, helping to keep you grounded when life gets stormy.

As you step forward, remember to give yourself grace. There will be days when your energy is low or when a skill won't feel accessible. Progress is built over time through consistent, imperfect effort. Self-compassion and self-forgiveness are as important as any tool in this book. Revisit Chapter 8 when you need a reminder of how strong and vibrant you are.

You may be wondering, "Where do I go from here?" Here are a few ways to keep your momentum going:

* **Keep practicing your skills.** Choose one or two exercises from this book to return to regularly. Small, steady practice builds lasting change.
* **Stay connected.** Recovery is easier when you don't do it alone. Keep leaning on your support network. Join communities that share your values. Seek out therapy or peer support groups.
* **Create new experiences.** Cultivate opportunities for joy and connection. This step continues to expand your life beyond trauma.

Over time, these shifts will add up to a life you choose, not one shaped by survival. This is your story, and you decide how to write it.

Resources

BOOKS

The Finding Solid Ground Program Workbook: Overcoming Obstacles in Trauma Recovery—Hugo Schielke, Bethany Brand, and Ruth Lanius

The Complex PTSD Workbook: A Mind-Body Approach to Regaining Emotional Control and Becoming Whole—Arielle Schwartz

No Bad Parts: Healing Trauma and Restoring Wholeness with the Internal Family Systems Model—Richard Schwartz

Getting Past Your Past: Take Control of Your Life with Self-Help Techniques from EMDR Therapy—Francine Shapiro

Body-First Healing: Get Unstuck and Recover from Trauma with Somatic Healing—Brittany Piper

Complex PTSD: From Surviving to Thriving—Pete Walker

It's Not Always Depression: Working the Change Triangle to Listen to the Body, Discover Core Emotions, and Connect to Your Authentic Self—Hilary Jacobs Hendel

PODCASTS

Complex Trauma Recovery—Kina Penelope

Trauma Rewired—Jennifer Wallace

The Healing Trauma Podcast—Monique Koven

WEBSITES AND ONLINE COMMUNITIES

Trauma-Sensitive Yoga: traumasensitiveyoga.com

Meetup: meetup.com (local interest or support groups)

Eventbrite: eventbrite.com (workshops, wellness events, and community gatherings)

Multiplied By One: multipliedbyone.org/did-resources/#PTSD (Dissociative Identity Disorder [DID] and PTSD resources)

CPTSD Foundation: cptsdfoundation.org

Out of the Storm: outofthestorm.website

Hilary Jacobs Hendel: hilaryjacobshendel.com

APPS

How We Feel (daily mood tracking and emotional literacy)

Urge Surf (support for navigating urges in a mindful way)

Open Breathwork/Meditation (nervous system regulation-informed guided meditations, breathwork, yoga, and stretching)

SUPPORT LINES (UNITED STATES)

988 Suicide and Crisis Lifeline—call or text 988

Substance Abuse and Mental Health Services Administration (SAMHSA) Helpline—1-800-662-HELP (4357)

Rape, Abuse & Incest National Network (RAINN) Hotline—1-800-656-4673 | online.rainn.org

National Domestic Violence Hotline—1-800-799-SAFE (7233) | text "START" to 88788

Appendix

Safety Plan

This plan is meant to help you stay safe and grounded during moments of distress, overwhelm, or crisis. It can be completed with or without a therapist, and you can revisit or revise it as your needs change.

1. **Early Warning Signs**

   How I can tell I'm beginning to feel unsafe or dysregulated.

   Physical cues: ______________________________

   ____

   ____

   Emotional cues: ______________________________

   ____

   ____

   Thought patterns: ______________________________

   ____

   ____

   Behaviors I notice in myself: ______________________________

   ____

   ____

   Examples: racing heart, feeling trapped, thinking "I can't do this," withdrawing, skipping meals

2. **Grounding and Self-Soothing Tools**
   Steps I can take on my own to lower distress and reconnect with safety.

   Breath or body practices that help me regulate: ______________________

   ____

   Comforting sensory tools (touch, smell, sound, etc.): ______________________

   ____

   Reassuring reminders, mantras, or self-talk: ______________________

   ____

   Environments or activities that bring calm: ______________________

   ____

   Examples: slow exhales, holding an ice cube, walking outside, listening to calming music

3. **Reaching Out for Connection**
   People I can contact when I need support.

Name	Relationship	Phone/Contact	How they can help

4. **Safe Environments**

Places I can go—or things I can do—to create physical or emotional safety.

Safe spaces (*home, friend's house, favorite public space*): ______________________

____

____

Calming rituals or routines: ______________________________

____

____

Things that make my space feel safer (*lighting, music, weighted blanket*):

____

____

____

5. **Reasons for Living**

What keeps me connected to life when things feel unbearable.

People or pets who matter to me: ___________________________

____

Responsibilities or goals I care about: _______________________

____

Beliefs, values, or hopes that ground me: _____________________

____

____

Examples: "I want to see my niece grow up," "My clients count on me," "I'm still healing."

6. **Professional and Crisis Support**

If the above steps aren't enough, these are the next resources to turn to.

My therapist/clinician: ______________________________

Psychiatry or medical contact: ______________________________

24-HOUR SUPPORT LINES:

* 988 Suicide & Crisis Lifeline (US): Call or text 988
* Crisis Text Line: Text HOME to 741741
* Trans Lifeline: 877-565-8860
* If outside the US: Find international hotlines here: findahelpline.com, or search online for your country's local helpline.

7. **Safety Commitments**

What I will do to protect myself when I notice risk increasing.

- ☐ Remove or secure items I could use to harm myself.
- ☐ Avoid alcohol or substances that increase impulsivity.
- ☐ Use my plan and reach out before acting on unsafe thoughts.
- ☐ Go to the nearest emergency department if I cannot stay safe.

Signature ______________________________

Date ______________________________

References

Afari, N., Ahumada, S. M., Wright, L. J., Mostoufi, S., Golnari, G., Reis, V., & Cuneo, J. G. "Psychological Trauma and Functional Somatic Syndromes: A Systematic Review and Meta-Analysis." *Psychosomatic Medicine*, 76, no. 1 (2014), 2–11. https://doi.org/10.1097/PSY.0000000000000010

American Psychiatric Association. *Diagnostic and Statistical Manual of Mental Disorders* (5th ed., text rev.; DSM-5-TR). American Psychiatric Publishing, 2022.

American Psychological Association. (2023). "Gaslight." In *APA Dictionary of Psychology*. https://dictionary.apa.org/gaslight

American Psychological Association. *Guidelines for Working with Adults with Complex Trauma Histories*. 2024. https://www.apa.org/practice/guidelines/adults-complex-trauma-histories.pdf

Becker, D., & Lamb, S. "Sex Bias in the Diagnosis of Borderline Personality Disorder and Posttraumatic Stress Disorder." *Professional Psychology: Research and Practice*, 25, no. 1 (1994): 55–61. https://doi.org/10.1037/0735-7028.25.1.55

Biro, F. M., & Deardorff, J. "Identifying Opportunities for Cancer Prevention During Preadolescence and Adolescence: Puberty as a Window of Susceptibility." *The Journal of Adolescent Health: Official Publication of the Society for Adolescent Medicine*, 52, no. 5, Suppl (2013): S15–S20. https://doi.org/10.1016/j.jadohealth.2012.09.019

Boon, S., Steele, K., & van der Hart, O. *Coping with Trauma-Related Dissociation: Skills Training for Patients and Therapists*. W. W. Norton & Company, 2011.

Bremner, J. D. "Traumatic Stress: Effects on the Brain." *Dialogues in Clinical Neuroscience*, 8, no. 4 (2006): 445–461. https://www.ncbi.nlm.nih.gov/pmc/articles/PMC3181836/

Brom, D., Stokar, Y., Lawi, C., Nuriel-Porat, V., Ziv, Y., Lerner, K., & Ross, G. "Somatic Experiencing for Posttraumatic Stress Disorder: A Randomized Controlled Outcome Study." *Journal of Traumatic Stress*, 30, no. 3 (2017): 304–312. https://doi.org/10.1002/jts.22189

Cacioppo, J. T., & Cacioppo, S. "Social Relationships and Health: The Toxic Effects of Perceived Social Isolation." *Social and Personality Psychology Compass*, 8, no. 2 (2014): 58–72. https://doi.org/10.1111/spc3.12087

Chapman, A. L. "Dialectical Behavior Therapy: Current Indications and Unique Elements." *Psychiatry* (Edgmont), 3, no. 9 (2006): 62–68.

Church, D. "Clinical EFT as an Evidence-Based Practice for the Treatment of Psychological and Physiological Conditions." *Psychology*, 4, no. 8 (2013): 645–654. https://www.scirp.org/journal/paperinformation.aspx?paperid=35751

Cloitre, M., Hyland, P., Bisson, J. I., Brewin, C. R., Roberts, N., Karatzias, T., & Shevlin, M. "ICD-11 Posttraumatic Stress Disorder and Complex Posttraumatic Stress Disorder in the United States: A Population-Based Study." *Journal of Traumatic Stress*, 32, no. 6 (2019): 833–842. https://doi.org/10.1002/jts.22454

Comeau, A., Smith, L. J., Smith, L., Soumerai Rea, H., Ward, M. C., Creedon, T. B., Sweezy, M., Rosenberg, L. G., & Schuman-Olivier, Z. "Online Group-Based Internal Family Systems Treatment for Posttraumatic Stress Disorder: Feasibility and Acceptability of the Program for Alleviating and Resolving Trauma and Stress." *Psychological Trauma: Theory, Research, Practice, and Policy*, 16, Suppl 3 (2024): S636–S640. https://doi.org/10.1037/tra0001688

Comninos, Andreas. "Expanding Your Window of Tolerance: 5 Strategies for Coping and Resilience." Mindfulness & Clinical Psychology Solutions, https://mi-psych.com.au/understanding-your-window-of-tolerance.

Damis, L. F. "The Role of Implicit Memory in the Development and Recovery from Trauma-Related Disorders." *NeuroSci*, 3, no. 1 (2022): 63–88. https://doi.org/10.3390/neurosci3010005

Dana, D. *The Polyvagal Theory in Therapy: Engaging the Rhythm of Regulation*. W. W. Norton & Company, 2018.

Fraser, G. A. "The Dissociative Table Technique: A Strategy for Working with Ego States in Dissociative Disorders and Ego-State Therapy." *Dissociation: Progress in the Dissociative Disorders*, 4, no. 4 (1991): 205–213.

Gordon, E. M., Chauvin, R. J., Van, A. N., Rajesh, A., Nielsen, et al. "A Somato-Cognitive Action Network Alternates with Effector Regions in Motor Cortex." *Nature*, 617, no. 7960 (2023): 351–359. https://doi.org/10.1038/s41586-023-05964-2

Haslam, S. A., Jetten, J., Postmes, T., & Haslam, C. "Social Identity, Health and Well-Being: An Emerging Agenda for Applied Psychology." *Applied Psychology: An International Review*, 58, no. 1 (2009): 1–23. https://doi.org/10.1111/j.1464-0597.2008.00379.x

Hayes, S. C., Strosahl, K. D., & Wilson, K. G. *Acceptance and Commitment Therapy: The Process and Practice of Mindful Change* (2nd ed.). Guilford Press, 2011.

Hendel, H. J. *It's Not Always Depression: Working the Change Triangle to Listen to the Body, Discover Core Emotions, and Connect to Your Authentic Self.* Penguin Random House, 2018.

Herman, J. L. *Trauma and Recovery: The Aftermath of Violence—From Domestic Abuse to Political Terror.* Basic Books, 1992.

Hinojosa, H. A., et al. "Exaggerated Amygdala Activation to Ambiguous Facial Expressions Is a Familial Vulnerability Factor for Posttraumatic Stress Disorder." *Journal of Psychiatric Research*, 156 (2023): 451–495. https://doi.org/10.1016/j.jpsychires.2022.10.049

Hodgdon, H. B., Anderson, F. G., Southwell, E., Hrubec, W., & Schwartz, R. "Internal Family Systems (IFS) Therapy for Posttraumatic Stress Disorder (PTSD) Among Survivors of Multiple Childhood Trauma: A Pilot Effectiveness Study." *Journal of Aggression, Maltreatment & Trauma*, 31, no. 1 (2022): 22–43. https://doi.org/10.1080/10926771.2021.2013375

Inami, T., Shimizu, T., Baba, R., & Nakagaki, A. "Acute Changes in Autonomic Nerve Activity During Passive Static Stretching." *American Journal of Sports Science and Medicine*, 2, vol. 4 (2014): 166–170. https://doi.org/10.12691/ajssm-2-4-9

Invitto, S., & Moselli, P. "Exploring Embodied and Bioenergetic Approaches in Trauma Therapy: Observing Somatic Experience and Olfactory Memory." *Brain Sciences*, 14, no. 4 (2024): 385. https://doi.org/10.3390/brainsci14040385

Knipe, J. *EMDR Toolbox: Theory and Treatment of Complex PTSD and Dissociation* (2nd ed.). Springer Publishing Company, 2018.

Levine, P. A. *Waking the Tiger: Healing Trauma*. North Atlantic Books, 1997.

Liberzon, I., & Sripada, C. S. "The Functional Neuroanatomy of PTSD: A Critical Review." *Progress in Brain Research*, 167 (2007): 151–169. https://doi.org/10.1016/S0079-6123(07)67011-3

Linehan, M. M. *DBT® Skills Training Manual* (2nd ed.). Guilford Press, 2014.

Logan, J. G., & Yeo, S. "Effects of Stretching Exercise on Heart Rate Variability During Pregnancy." *Journal of Cardiovascular Nursing*, 32, no. 2 (2017): 107–111. https://doi.org/10.1097/JCN.0000000000000326

Lucas, A. R., Klepin, H. D., Porges, S. W., & Rejeski, W. J. "Mindfulness-Based Movement: A Polyvagal Perspective." *Integrative Cancer Therapies*, 17, no. 1 (2018): 5–15. https://doi.org/10.1177/1534735416682087

McLeod, S. (n.d.). "Maslow's Hierarchy of Needs." *SimplyPsychology*. Retrieved July 9, 2025, from https://www.simplypsychology.org/maslow.html

Neff, K. *Self-Compassion: The Proven Power of Being Kind to Yourself.* William Morrow, 2011.

Neimeyer, R. A., Herrero, O., & Botella, L. "Chaos to Coherence: Psychotherapeutic Integration of Traumatic Loss." *Journal of Constructivist Psychology*, 19, no. 2 (2006): 127–145. https://doi.org/10.1080/10720530500508738

Norcross, J. C., & Lambert, M. J. "Psychotherapy Relationships that Work III." *Psychotherapy*, 55, no. 4 (2018): 303–315. https://doi.org/10.1037/pst0000193

Ogden, P., & Fisher, J. *Sensorimotor Psychotherapy: Interventions for Trauma and Attachment* (Norton Series on Interpersonal Neurobiology). W. W. Norton & Company, 2015.

Okoh, L. "Determining the Effectiveness of Deep Breathing Exercises in Alleviating Stress in Veterans with Post-Traumatic Stress Disorder (PTSD)" (Doctor of Nursing Practice scholarly project, Arkansas State University). Arkansas State University Digital Archive. (2024) https://arch.astate.edu/dnp-projects/78

Özcan, N. "The Effectiveness of Somatic Experience Based Stabilization Program for Refugee Women's Post-Traumatic Stress, Mindfulness and Social Support Level." *Psycho-Educational Research Reviews*, 10, no. 1 (2021): 46–60.

Paulsen, S. L., & O'Shea, K. M. "When There Are No Words: Repairing Early Trauma and Neglect from the Attachment Period with EMDR Therapy." CreateSpace Independent Publishing Platform, 2017.

Pennebaker, J. W., & Beall, S. K. "Confronting a Traumatic Event: Toward an Understanding of Inhibition and Disease." *Journal of Abnormal Psychology*, 95, no. 3 (1986): 274–281. https://doi.org/10.1037/0021-843X.95.3.274

Pennebaker, J. W., & Smyth, J. M. *Opening Up by Writing It Down: How Expressive Writing Improves Health and Eases Emotional Pain* (3rd ed.). Guilford Press, 2016.

Pham, L. B., & Taylor, S. E. "From Thought to Action: Effects of Process- Versus Outcome-Based Mental Simulations on Performance." *Personality and Social Psychology Bulletin*, 25, no. 2 (1999): 250–260. https://doi.org/10.1177/0146167299025002010

Porges, S. W. "The Polyvagal Perspective." *Biological Psychology*, 74, no. 2 (2007): 116–143. https://doi.org/10.1016/j.biopsycho.2006.06.009

Porges, S. W. *The Polyvagal Theory: Neurophysiological Foundations of Emotions, Attachment, Communication, and Self-Regulation*. W. W. Norton & Company, 2011.

Porter, C., Palmier-Claus, J., Branitsky, A., Mansell, W., Warwick, H., & Varese, F. "Childhood Adversity and Borderline Personality Disorder: A Meta-Analysis." *ActaPsychiatrica Scandinavica*, 141, no. 1 (2020): 6–20. https://doi.org/10.1111/acps.13118

Ravi, M., Mekawi, Y., Blevins, E. J., Michopoulos, V., Stevens, J., Carter, S., & Powers, A. "Intersections of Oppression: Examining the Interactive Effect of Racial Discrimination and Neighborhood Poverty on PTSD Symptoms in Black Women." *Journal of Psychopathology and Clinical Science*, 132, no. 5 (2023): 567–576. https://doi.org/10.1037/abn0000818

Resick, P. A., Monson, C. M., & Chard, K. M. *Cognitive Processing Therapy for PTSD: A Comprehensive Manual.* Guilford Press, 2016.

Rothschild, B. *The Body Remembers: The Psychophysiology of Trauma and Trauma Treatment*. W. W. Norton & Company, 2000.

Samulowitz, A., Gremyr, I., Eriksson, E., & Hensing, G. "'Brave Men' and 'Emotional Women': A Theory-Guided Literature Review on Gender Bias in Health Care and Gendered Norms Towards Patients with Chronic Pain." *Pain Research and Management* (2018). https://doi.org/10.1155/2018/6358624

Schielke, H. J., Brand, B. L., & Lanius, R. A. *The Finding Solid Ground Program Workbook: Overcoming Obstacles in Trauma Recovery*. Oxford University Press, 2022.

Schnurr, P. P., & Green, B. L. "Understanding Relationships Among Trauma, Post-Traumatic Stress Disorder, and Health Outcomes." *Advances in Mind-Body Medicine*, 20, no. 1 (2004): 18–29. https://pubmed.ncbi.nlm.nih.gov/15068106/

Schwartz, A. *The Complex PTSD Workbook: A Mind-Body Approach to Regaining Emotional Control and Becoming Whole* (Workbook ed.). Callisto Publishing, 2017.

Schwartz, R. C. *Internal Family Systems Therapy*. Guilford Press, 1995.

Shapiro, F. *Getting Past Your Past: Take Control of Your Life with Self-Help Techniques from EMDR Therapy*. Rodale, 2012.

Shin, L., & Liberzon, I. "The Neurocircuitry of Fear, Stress, and Anxiety Disorders." *Neuropsychopharmacology*, 35 (2010): 169–191. https://doi.org/10.1038/npp.2009.83

Smith, M. E. "Bilateral Hippocampal Volume Reduction in Adults with Post-Traumatic Stress Disorder: A Meta-Analysis of Structural MRI Studies." *Hippocampus*, 15, no. 6 (2005): 798–807. https://doi.org/10.1002/hipo.20102

Stanley, B., & Brown, G. K. "Safety Planning Intervention: A Brief Intervention to Mitigate Suicide Risk." *Cognitive and Behavioral Practice*, 19, no. 2 (2012): 256–264. https://doi.org/10.1016/j.cbpra.2011.01.001

Stark, E. *Coercive Control: How Men Entrap Women in Personal Life*. Oxford University Press, 2007.

Steger, M. F., Shin, J. Y., Shim, Y., & Fitch-Martin, A. "Is Meaning in Life a Flagship Indicator of Well-Being?" In A. S. Waterman (Ed.), *The Best Within Us: Positive Psychology Perspectives on Eudaimonia* (159–182). American Psychological Association, 2013. https://doi.org/10.1037/14092-009

Sweet, P. L. "The Sociology of Gaslighting." *American Sociological Review*, 84, no. 5 (2019). 851–875. https://doi.org/10.1177/0003122419874843

Tang, Y., & Tang, R. "How the Brain/Mind and Body Affect our Health Behavior and Outcomes." *Journal of Integrative Neuroscience*, 23, no. 4 (2024): 69. https://doi.org/10.31083/j.jin2304069

Tedeschi, R. G., & Calhoun, L. G. "Posttraumatic Growth: Conceptual Foundations and Empirical Evidence." *Psychological Inquiry*, 15, no. 1 (2004): 1–18. https://doi.org/10.1207/s15327965pli1501_01

Tolin, D. F., & Foa, E. B. "Sex Differences in Trauma and Posttraumatic Stress Disorder: A Quantitative Review of 25 Years of Research." *Psychological Bulletin*, 132, no. 6 (2006): 959–992. https://doi.org/10.1037/0033-2909.132.6.959

Tomaszewski, C., Belot, R.-A., Essadek, A., Onumba-Bessonnet, H., & Clesse, C. "Therapeutic Impact of Dance Therapy on Adult Individuals with Psychological Trauma: A Systematic Review." medRxiv. (2022). https://doi.org/10.1101/2022.10.27.22281614

van der Kolk, B. A. "The Body Keeps the Score: Memory and the Evolving Psychobiology of Posttraumatic Stress." *Harvard Review of Psychiatry*, 1, no. 5 (1994): 253–265. https://doi.org/10.3109/10673229409017088

van der Kolk, B. A. *The Body Keeps the Score: Brain, Mind, and Body in the Healing of Trauma.* Penguin Books, 2015.

van der Kolk, B. A., Stone, L., West, J., Rhodes, A., Emerson, D., Suvak, M., & Spinazzola, J. "Yoga as an Adjunctive Treatment for Posttraumatic Stress Disorder: A Randomized Controlled Trial." *Journal of Clinical Psychiatry*, 75, no. 6 (2014): e559–e565.

Walker, L. E. *The Battered Woman*. Harper and Row, 1979.

Walker, P. *Complex PTSD: From Surviving to Thriving: A Guide and Map for Recovering from Childhood Trauma*. Azure Coyote Books, 2013.

Waxenbaum, J. A., Reddy, V., & Varacallo, M. "Anatomy, Autonomic Nervous System." StatPearls. StatPearls Publishing, 2023. https://www.ncbi.nlm.nih.gov/books/NBK539845/

"What Is EFT Tapping?" (n.d.). Yogaressa. Retrieved July 8, 2025, from https://yogaressa.com/what-is-eft-tapping/

World Health Organization. *International Classification of Diseases for Mortality and Morbidity Statistics* (11th ed.). 2019. https://icd.who.int/

Yehuda, R. "Biology of Posttraumatic Stress Disorder." *The Journal of Clinical Psychiatry*, 62, Suppl 17 (2001): 41–46.

Yuan, Y., Lee, H., Eack, S. M., & Newhill, C. E. "A Systematic Review of the Association Between Early Childhood Trauma and Borderline Personality Disorder." *Journal of Personality Disorders*, 37, no. 1 (2023): 16–35. https://doi.org/10.1521/pedi.2023.37.1.16

Zaccari, B., Higgins, M., Haywood, T. N., West, J., Emerson, D., Suvak, M., & Spinazzola, J. "Yoga vs Cognitive Processing Therapy for Military Sexual Trauma–Related Posttraumatic Stress Disorder: A Randomized Clinical Trial." JAMA Network Open, 6(12), e2344862. (2023) https://doi.org/10.1001/jamanetworkopen.2023.44862

Index

Acknowledgments

I'd like to begin by acknowledging the incredible team at Penguin Random House—Tahra Seplowin, for first contacting me with this idea; Carolyn Abate, Shara Underweiser, and Christina MacDonald, for their thoughtful contributions; and most important, my editor, Erin Nelson, for trusting me with this project and walking alongside me through every stage, helping bring it to life.

Thank you to my team at The Manhattan Psychotherapy Collective. You are all my biggest cheerleaders, and I am eternally grateful for your support. Not everyone is as lucky to have a team like this one.

My sincere appreciation goes to my consultants throughout the years—Pria Alpern, Esther Goldstein, and Wendy Freitag—whose clinical wisdom and guidance have shaped the way I practice trauma therapy.

Thank you to my husband, Ross, and my parents for their unwavering support and faith in me—no matter the idea or project I've decided to take on.

Finally, thank you to my clients. This book is informed by all I have learned from you. You know who you are.

About the Author

DEBBIE MISSUD, LMHC-D, is a licensed psychotherapist and founder of The Manhattan Psychotherapy Collective, a group practice in New York City specializing in trauma-informed care for women. She works primarily with clients navigating complex trauma, anxiety, and attachment wounds, and is certified in EMDR with advanced training in integrative modalities including IFS, DBT, and somatic therapies.

In addition to her therapy practice, Debbie provides clinical supervision and consultation for mental health professionals. Beyond the therapy room, she's a mental health educator on social media, known as @therapydebbie, where she blends expertise with humor and humanity to make healing concepts relatable and accessible. She's passionate about bridging the gap between clinical knowledge and everyday life, helping people better understand themselves and their relationships.

When she's not working, Debbie can be found walking her dog through the city, experimenting in the kitchen, flowing through a hot yoga class, or enjoying evenings with friends over great food and conversation. She believes that healing isn't just about what happens in therapy—it's also about the joy, connection, and meaning we create outside of it.

Reset your nervous system and foster resilience with this soothing science-backed deck

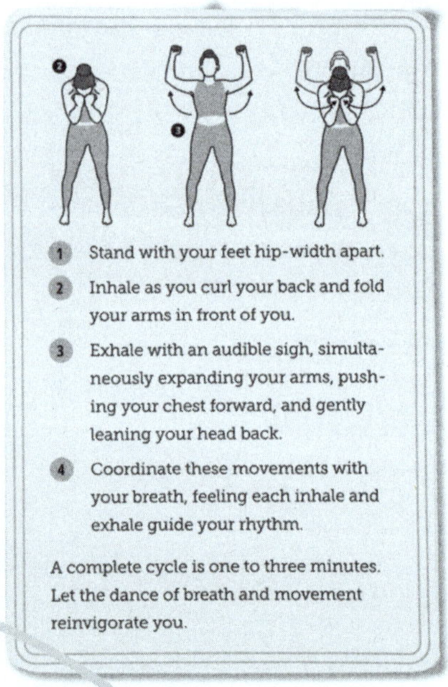

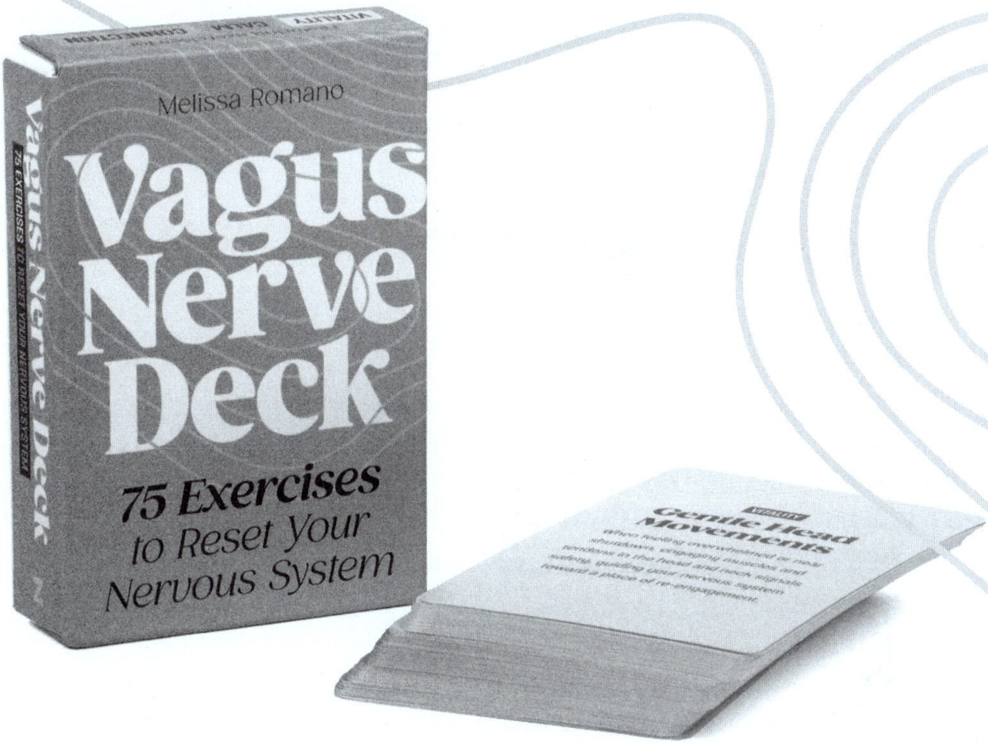
Melissa Romano
Vagus Nerve Deck
75 Exercises to Reset Your Nervous System
Gentle Head Movements

Hi there,

We hope you found *Self-Directed Complex PTSD Exercises for Women* helpful. If you have any questions or concerns about your book, or have received a damaged copy, please contact customerservice@penguinrandomhouse.com. We're here and happy to help.

Also, please consider writing a review on your favorite retailer's website to let others know what you thought of the book.

Sincerely,

The Zeitgeist Team